LEAPING
into the SKY

ROBERT LIVINGSTON

Executive Press Ltd
Edmonton AB T6A 0H7
Canada
343-554-1210

The views expressed in this work are solely those of the author and do not necessarily reflect
the views of the publisher, and the publisher hereby disclaims any responsibility for them.

Paperback ISBN: 979-8-9913174-6-7
Ebook ISBN: 979-8-9913174-7-4

Leaping Into
The Sky

Robert Livingston

OTHER BOOKS BY ROBERT LIVINGSTON

THE SAILOR AND THE TEACHER

TRAVELS WITH ERNIE

LEAPING INTO THE SKY

BLUE JACKETS

FLEET

HARLEM ON THE WESTERN FRONT

W.T. STEAD AND THE CONSPIRACY OF
1910 TO SAVE THE WORLD

IN THE WAKE OF THE EMPRESS OF CHINA

THE FORGOTTEN CHAPLAIN

AXIS SALLY

THE TARNISHED ROSE

AMERICAN STORIES 1940 - 1960

THE ANCHOR AND THE JOURNALIST

TASTE THE WIND

A DEAN'S LIFE

A FEW SPECIAL WORDS

Happy Birthday Garvey, today you are celebrating your sixteenth birthday. If I calculated correctly, today is May 11, 2030 and you are a junior in high school taking U.S. History among other subjects.

As requested, your parents are giving you a present from me today, a story I wrote in 2012. I wrote this story for you with a single purpose in mind. I wanted you to know about the issue of "race" in American life and about young men who over came bigotry and discrimination in their lives. To do so, I selected a topic in American history generally not discussed in high school, or even in colleges and universities.

Your story is entitled *Leaping into the Sky.* In the narrative you are attending Woodrow Wilson High School in Seattle. Your U.S. History teacher required a term paper. Unsure of a topic you talk to your grandfather (that's me). At his urging you decide to write about young Black men in the American Army during World War II (1941 – 1945). Specifically, your research will be about the men of the 555th Airborne. Why this topic? As you will learn these "men of color," all but forgotten in our history books, sacrificed everything for human freedom and personal dignity by jumping out of airplanes at a time when racial prejudice was all too common in America and certainly in the military.

In this story, Garvey, you will travel to Oregon and Kansas to unearth a long neglected slice of American history. You will do so with your grandfather, whom you call "Gramps." Together the two of you will have a wild ride through the past as you uncover the story behind the Army's experiment to create an all-Black airborne unit at a time when Blacks were systematically denied combat roles.

Aspects of these stories will not be enjoyable. You will learn about racism in America. The "ugliness" of this history is just that. No cleaning agent can fully eradicate this stain of the past. However, by confronting this history it is possible to learn about the past and to make peace with it. And that is important as all of us struggle to make a better America for all of our people.

For me, it was a joy to be with you in your sixteenth year of life as a literary companion in this story. I enjoyed every moment we spent together as I thought of you while writing about the "men who leaped into the sky."

With love and affection,

Gramps,
2018

Contents

CHAPTER I

THE JUMP

MAY, 1945 – NORTHERN CALIFORNIA

Late Afternoon

The venerable C-47 forestry plane, buffeted by violent updrafts and vicious cross-winds, flew low through the morning skies, laced with haze and drifting smoke, which gave the rising sun in the east an ugly, blood-red dirty look, and the promise of a long, difficult day fighting an uncontrolled wild fire.

Though they were unaware of it the military occupants of the aircraft were about to make history. Unfortunately, the U.S. Army deemed the secret flight a matter of national security. The general public was not informed of this flight, nor would it be over the next four decades.

High above the plane the lightning-filled clouds of the night's passing storm still colored the sky with departing smudges of inky-gray galleons. Gone, too, were Thor's bolts of incandescent light, streaking downward and lighting up the night with spears of electrically charged particles seeking, as if drawn by some powerful magnet, the tallest strand of spruce or ponderosa trees.

In the storm's aftermath little was left beyond the plane, the horizon, and the tree-dotted mountains below.

1

Lightning strikes, thought Jake Turner, I'll never get used to them. Truth be told, I hate them. They scare the hell out of me. Piloting a metal, two-engine cargo plan toward a lightning strike was like playing Russian roulette with Mother Nature. Do it enough times and one of her "bolts" is liable to wing you. And why do the strikes almost always occur in the most remote mountain areas, where only deer and bears can move freely and passable roads are almost non-existent. And the guys harnessed behind me… Poor bastards. Once they leap out they'll be hit by drenching rain cascading down, driven by bone-chilling blustering winds.

But it was a job. It was my job, Jake reminded himself. And now these guys dressed in fatigues… Pretty soon it would be their job. Tough way to make a living…

The alarm, the cry to battle, he recalled, almost always began the same way. A storm, as predicted by the weather boys, arrived high over Humboldt County just south of the Oregon border along the California coast. Driven southward from Alaska the maelstrom battered through the sky pelting those below with lightning and thunder, and a torrent of rain. And then, as always, the reports came in from the lonely lookouts, "Smoke column at … Then the coordinates would be given, longitude and latitude sufficient information to pin-point a potential lightning strike on forestry maps. That's the way it always started this unceasing struggle with the elements.

DOUGLAS C-47

<u>Earlier</u>

In a well-rehearsed routine, Jake had flown the old single-engine U.S. Forestry spotter plane into the fire area, flying low and alone, connected to the world by radio only, a latter day "Lone Eagle." He loved the freedom of flight and accepted the obligations and risks that fire spotting entailed. Better than selling shoes at Sears, he thought, or refrigerators at Monkey Ward. That was for others. He belonged in the air.

And then Jake saw it off in the distance. Jackpot! Smoke column right where the lookouts had said. The strike appears to be less than an acre, but slowly growing in heavy foliage and surrounded by tall ponderosa. Very steep terrain. There's a possible drop site 500-yards south of fire. Small clearing, possibly a mountain meadow… And then… "I see it!" Jake said, a shrill to his usually calm voice. "Repeat, I see it! One of them, I'm sure. It's hanging from a ponderosa, 50-feet off the ground. No doubt about it. The basket is still tied to the balloon." And then with his voice rising, "the incendiaries are still hanging from basket. Looks like at least five. Fire encroaching slowly uphill on the basket; this will not be a drill. Repeat, not a drill!"

THE BALLOON BOMB

——————————

Three hours ago, Jake reflected, he had spotted the fire and the thing. Army Intelligence had been right. The written alert he received two months ago in a brown envelope was marked TOP SECRET... Alive in the jet stream at 30,000 feet the balloon weapons were crossing the Pacific, the Army stated, traveling eastward toward the American northwest. Further calculations by the Army had, after considering wind, course, and speed, projected landfalls in Northern California, Oregon, and Washington State, each an unsolicited gift from the Emperor of Japan. Unsolicited, Jake reminded himself, as was Iwo Jima, Okinawa, and the looming invasion of Japan.

Now here he was, Jake thought to himself, wading through the turbulent morning sky in the C-47 with 17-guys depending on him to get them to the drop zone. That was his job. Get these young men safely to where the column of smoke indicated a lightning strike. The drop zone ... A stamp-size piece of real estate near where the "thing" was hanging in the trees, apparently and suspiciously mute but inherently dangerous. Knowing all this, Jake didn't envy what his passengers were up against once they jumped. Fighting a forest fire was one thing. Man versus nature. Jumpers understood the inherent risks. But this was something else. The deadly and vicious Pacific war in the forests of the northwest... Who would have thought it possible?

Earlier, once he had made his "report," there had hardly been time to land his spotter plane on the airstrip assigned to the US Forestry Service, throw down some questionable, liquidity scrambled eggs and two cups of thick black coffee before scampering to the C-47 at the airport. At least, what the town of Chico, California called an airport. No offense intended. Moments later he was in the cockpit, checking his instruments and getting last minute weather information. He revved up the engines until they were straining to career down the runway, fulfilling the natural instinct of the C-47 to fly, to break the grip of earthly gravity, and to soar above land.

It all sounded so romantic in the books and on the movie screen, Jake thought. Heroic pilot challenging nature, the handsome, courageous pilot flying high above the Pacific Mountain Range determined to complete his mission. Hollywood would have provided a full orchestra and grandiose music as the pilot and plane loaded down with men and equipment, took to the skies to challenge the unwelcome invader. Yeah! Where was John Ford when you needed him?

Jake had waited for the guys, each heavily weighted down with equipment, and wearing a thick smokejumper's outfit, to climb awkwardly into the plane. Not like the Marines climbing down cargo swinging nets into a waiting Higgins boat for the frightful run to the beach, but still dangerous. Not like that at all. These guys, his guys, were newly trained and out to prove something. They had a large chip on their shoulders. Who could blame them after what they had endured. They would hit the hostile beach from 2500 feet high, dangling from a silk canopy against an enemy devoid of human compassion. They were in the Army. They were smokejumpers. That was their destiny.

ARMY SMOKEJUMPERS – 1945

The cabin had door closed. Everyone was aboard and seated, two long rows of silent men facing each other. Brake blocks were removed from the wheels. The radio announced: "clear for takeoff." It was time to throttle back, Jake knew. He had done it a hundred times, but never with this human cargo. The C-47 lugged itself down the rain-soaked runway spraying water in every direction before, ever so slowly rising into the "Wild Blue Yonder."

———————

That was then, Jake thought, but this is now. Time to check the coordinates. Got to locate the fire, and the green mountain meadow, he reminded himself, and the drop site. These guys depend on me. I'm their best hope for a clean jump.

Focus on the horizon. Do your job. Reach out with your eyes, Jake told himself, and let years of experience gained flying help you, first in barnstorming events back in the early 30's and later climbing over the "hump" in Burma to ferry war supplies to China for Uncle Sam. If a Jap Zero hadn't knocked him out of the sky, he recalled with anger, he might still be "flying. But he had survived the crash landing, though severely injured, and the three weeks of eluding the enemy in the jungle before being rescued by friendly natives. Much luckier than some of his buddies, he knew. After a tour of two V.A. hospitals, he was mustered out of the service because of his injuries. Back in the civilian world and looking for work. Then a job as a "cargo jockey" for the U.S. Forestry Service came his way. The hours were crazy but the pay was enough to survive on. That was okay. He was still doing what he loved. He was flying.

And now these guys, his new pals by chance. It had been quite a surprise when he first met them. And then, when he learned what their real task was he had been taken aback. Time and training had created a healthy respect for these guys, not only for each other, but also the task at hand.

Jake eyed the horizon. Just keep your wits about you, he reminded himself again. Just do your job.

Next to Jake sat John O'Brien, a career Forestry Ranger, almost at retirement age and stationed in Chico, not far from Sacramento, the state capital of California. Fought with Marines under Pershing in

President Wilson's earlier war to "make the world safe for democracy." He was too old for the sequel, but not this last wrinkle of the present conflagration. Unlike the slim, lanky Jake, O'Brien was a thick, heavyset man, carrying over 200 pounds in his olive-green forestry uniform. And still tough as nails.

They made a fine pair, the pilot and the Ranger.

Binoculars in hand and pressed tightly against his heavily lined face, O'Brien strained his eyes peering through the plane's windshield for the elusive young fire and the desperately needed meadow high up in the Siskiyou National Forest. Can't give the order to jump, he reminded himself, until we find that drop site. Tiny it might be from the air, but still big enough for our needs. It had to be. An old Irish phrase escaped his lips. "God, protect all in this house." But this was an airborne house, he quickly said, yet the plea was still needed. "God, protect all in this plane, all on this mission." And then other words escaped. "Where are you?" he demanded. "Come on, show yourself. I know you're there. Don't play coy."

Behind the two men in the jump seat sat another man, very tall, very muscular, and very Army. Big Mike Thompson, a former pro-boxer. Once fought the "Bronx Bomber," Joe Louis. Went five rounds before the lights went out. Traded in boxing gloves for an M-1 to end Nazi atrocities in Europe and Japanese tyranny in China and throughout the western Pacific. Now he was a top sergeant. Not bad for a Negro kid from Mississippi whose linage traced back to slave days. Not easy, of course, for any Black in the U.S. Army in the 1940's with its racial attitudes.

Thompson was nervously leaning forward, searching ahead in his mind, his senses keyed to the job ahead. He was aware of his own anxiety, though he tried to hide it from the other men sitting behind him in the two long rows of the cargo bay. They already had enough to worry about. They sat silent. They stared straight ahead. They surmised the situation. They weren't stupid. They knew what was at stake. They waited. What else could they do? Past experience, and all the qualifying practices, told them to be patient. Time would pass.

THE MEN

Our first time, Thompson mused. There's always a first time. Finally, this was the real thing. Are we ready? Should I have prepared the men better? Will they freeze at the last second? No, scrub those thoughts. These guys will do what's expected of them. They've come so far. Beaten the odds, shattered the naysayers. They know what a successful jump will mean. This isn't just about a fire, or one of Nippon's gifts. That war could more easily be fought. They knew that. So much hung in the balance. Their lives, yes; but beyond that, their families and friends. So much to prove...

"Jesus," Thompson screamed quietly into his gloved hands, "where's that crummy piece of turf? A little help from above would be nice." Possibly a quiet prayer passed from his lips.

Thompson looked at his men. Eight jumpers on each side of the plane sat as erect as possible given their burdens. Each man was dressed, as was he, in heavy padded clothing, from his neck to his ankles. They all had thick boots on their feet and warm gloves encasing their hands to weathered the elements. On each head, but not yet his, a football helmet fit snugly, if not seemingly strangely out of place in the dreary cargo bay. Attached to each helmet was a strong wire mesh that completely obscured the face. Wired protection to protect the men from widow-makers among other dangers. A forerunner of the gridiron facemask future football players would wear. Already strapped to each man's back was an immense pack, which contained much that he would need: food, bedding, and tools. In the front was another pack, neatly and carefully packed as if a person's life depended on it. And, of course, it did. From the pack hung a cord. In time the cord would be attached to a long line, the jump cord. The front pack was crucial. It contained a parachute. The pack had the power of life and death.

All the occupants of the C-47 heard the constant, reassuring drone of the two powerful Pratt and Whitney R-1830 radial engines, each turning 2400 rpm, sufficient to power the propellers, which swished their way through the air, providing the lift that kept the old DC-3 aloft. No one cursed the droning of the engines and the whirl of the propellers.

DC-3... It was the original designation of the C-47 as a passenger plane before being converted for military purposes. The initials "DC" stood for "Douglas Commercial." Bring on a war, and like magic, "DC" becomes "C-47." From civilian use to military necessity with the snap of the government's fingers... As fate would have it, the prototype for the plane was first flown on December 17, 1935, which happened to be the 32nd anniversary of the Wright Brothers' flight at Kitty Hawk, North Carolina. Some coincidence...

Redesigned and renamed, the C-47 was the military cargo configuration of the craft, complete with a large cargo door and a strengthened floor to fend off anti-aircraft fire. In wartime it had made its way over the coast of Normandy, dropping paratroopers into France hours before the D-Day landings. In the vastness of the Pacific, especially in the New Guinea campaign, it had transported needed troops and supplies in the heat of battle. Later, from one bitterly fought island invasion to another, it had steadfastly done its job. What the jeep was to those on land, the C-47 was to those in the clouds, tough, dependable --- a "can do" creation of the good folks at Douglas Aircraft. It transported troops, cargo, the wounded, and the dead.

And now it was in a new war flying over the Pacific Coast Mountains of California.

"We should be on top of it by now," the Jake said matter-of-factly. "Right on top."

"What's our altitude, Jake?" the Ranger asked.

"4, triple 0. Don't want to run into a peak in this soup."

"Take her down to 2,500 feet. Carefully."

"10-4, and in one piece."

The plane banked left and rolled over into a slow downward descent. Visibility improved slightly as the plane slithered through smoke and mist before leveling out above a long-wooded alpine valley sandwiched between parallel columns of jagged, snow-capped mountain ridges.

"John, over there, at 3:00 o'clock."

"I see it," the Ranger exclaimed. "The smoke column right where you said it would be."

"Check for the clearing."

"There, just southeast of the fire."

"Christ," Thompson said to the Ranger, "that's our landing spot? That clearing?"

"All we have… And steep, too, Army," the Ranger replied quickly.

"If we miss the meadow…"

"Into the trees…"

Tough to land in tree, Thompson knew, as did his men. The ponderosa, so many of them, so damn tall with so many branches, all a natural obstacle. But the limbs were willowy. They might cushion a hard fall from the sky. But it would be difficult to rope down from them. And there might be rocks below. One false move… One mistake… Too many possibilities to consider; just depend on your training. Keep the faith.

Thompson's thoughts were interrupted. Jake was barking, "Would you look at that, just off to the right of the lightening strike. If things weren't tough enough already."

"Is that it?" asked the Ranger. "That mess in the trees?"

High in the ponderosa was a shimmering, whitish canopy, resembling a obscenely large parachute, no longer drifting through the sky, now collapsed and prostrate in the trees. Thanks to a gusting wind, folds of the material undulated, providing a rippling effect, and the appearance of life. No ghost was ever more frightening.

"Only thing it could be," Jake said. "Just like the photos the Army showed us.

"I see it, but where's the basket?" Thompson asked. "Where's the damn basket?"

"Not hanging in the trees," Jake cried. "Maybe the fire got to it."

"Sweet Jesus, is it on the ground?" the Ranger asked.

"Must be," Thompson said. "And lethal," he added. "Worse than the fire."

"Time to check the wind, guys," the Ranger said.

The Ranger moved cautiously from his seat to the cargo door, which he opened after donning goggles. Tightly gripping a door handle he looked out. He immediately felt the bracing cold air, which disguised the projected triple digit ground temperatures anticipated for the next day. Now he could see the ponderosas better. A spongy tree, he thought. Yes, it might break a jumper's fall if he got hung up in it. Still, would the branches be strong enough to permit a "let-down," roping your way to the ground?

"Bring her around, Jake. Time for the flares."

Quickly, the Ranger, now the "spotter," dropped five flares attached to small chutes. He watched the flares, judging from their descent both wind velocity and drift, important variables to consider. The lives of all the men depended on his judgment.

"Okay, for a jump run," he yelled.

"10-4," Jake quickly responded.

"Come in at 2000 feet."

The Jake throttled back on the engines, slowing the plane and then leveling off at the desired elevation. At the same time, Thompson roared, "hook up." One by one, the masked men connected themselves to the chute-line, their lifeline. A sharp tug, though bone-crunching at times, was what they lived for. No tug… Well, they didn't even consider that. No use dwelling on that possibility. No need to check their packs again. They had done that before lifting themselves into the C-47 back in Chico.

"Cut the engines back!" the Ranger yelled to the pilot.

"Cutting engines," Jake blurted out loudly. "Circling the landing site."

The Ranger needed one last look. Needed to double check… Needed to make sure…

"Next pass," he bellowed. Coming around. Get Ready."

The sergeant joined his men at the cargo bay door, enjoining them… "In groups of three. Okay, first group, jump."

One by one the men shuffled to the open cargo door, peered out, then leaped into the sky, and were gone. Thompson was the last to go, saying, "Thumbs up, guys."

Moments later … "Jumpers away," the Ranger yelled to Jake. "All away."

LEAPING INTO THE SKY

The Ranger watched the chutes open. Soon the sky was full of mushrooming chutes floating earthward. He counted under his breath. "Five, nine, twelve, fifteen, seventeen. All chutes open. No malfunctions."

"Time for the equipment runs, John," the pilot said. "Once the guys are on the ground."
"Okay."

The C-47 circled the jump site in a wide arc buying a few precious minutes of time.

"Ready, John?"
"They're down. Now."

The Ranger, now alone, manhandled bundles attached to parachutes, pushing them out the cargo door at just the right moment. Three bundles floated toward the drop site, all the additional supplies the men would have until they walked the eleven miles the small town of Elk Ridge once the fire was out. And once the "gift" from Japan was neutralized.

It was hard work pushing the bundles out. It was also geometry and physics at work, speed of the plane, drift of the wind, elevation of the plane, weight of the cargo, and rate of descent. So much depended on a successful cargo landing.

And it was dangerous work. As the Ranger heaved the last bundle into the morning sky, he lost his balance, and fell forward. Even as he fell, he grabbed a door brace, clinging to it with one hand as his feet dangled outside the plane.

Whether the Ranger yelled or screamed, it didn't matter. Jake heard him, took a quick look, and rolled the plane steeply over in the opposite direction. Gravity, the enemy a second ago, was now a friend. The Ranger fell back into the plane and grasped a metal strut in a protracted death grip. Catching his breath, he yelled, "Let's go home."

The plane righted itself, and then commenced a low pass over the drop site. As it passed the men on the ground, the pilot wagged the C-47's tail in token farewell before heading back to Chico. On the ground, the men silently waved back at the "gooney bird."

Now, cut off from the world, it was time to go to work. First the fire; put a fire line around the potential inferno. All done by hand; no mechanized equipment available. Work with a Pulaski, or a McCloud, and always with a shovel. Clean out hot spots. If present, cut down any snags. Axe time. And, stay away from the "basket" until it was time to disarm it. And keep the damn fire away from it. The sergeant reminded them of all this, exclaiming, "Let's do it. Uncle Sam isn't paying us to sit on our butts."

The men went to work.

Ten Days Later

The town of Elk Ridge, population 154 souls, wasn't much more than a grocery store with a gas pump, and a proprietor who was also the town mayor and local Post Master. There was one restaurant known for its salmon dinners and venison steaks. The owner, a relative of the mayor, was pretty good with eggs and potatoes too, if you were so inclined. The greasy burgers weren't bad, especially if you weren't counting calories. As for the black coffee, it was always thick, hot, and biting. But it was home brewed. The place catered to locals and the many fisherman and hunters who pounced on the town once it was time for the salmon run or the deer season.

On this particular day, two hunters were having breakfast. Both were from Alabama and the "deep South." They had been lured to the north by good paying jobs at Boeing, first in Seattle, and later in the San Francisco Bay Area. With the war coming to an end, they took a "hunting vacation," beer, guns, and no wives or kids for three days in the great outdoors. Sitting in the restaurant, their conversation was interrupted by a commotion outside.

"What's the excitement?" one yelled.

Standing in the doorway, the waitress said loudly, "Would you look at that?"

Another patron seconded her observation, almost shouting, "Now that's something you don't see every day."

Curious, the two hunters came to the doorway. Incredulity quickly covered their faces. In unison they said, "I don't believe it."

Others came out of the grocery store to see what was causing the disturbance, or something akin to it. Many stood open-mouthed at what they saw. "What the hell" was their general response."

Coming down the town's main street, its only street, were seventeen disheveled men wearing obviously worn and torn padded clothing, and carrying heavy loads on their backs. They wore helmets with wire mesh on them. The men walked in two straight lines, erectly and proudly, as if they were in the military and on parade. As they marched, they walked to a tight cadence, singing, "I left my wife in New Orleans with twenty-four kids and a can and beans. A left... A right... A left, right, left."

The leader of the men yelled, "Halt." The men stopped in front of the restaurant and waited for the next command. It quickly came. "At ease."

No one in Elk Ridge was more astonished than the two transplanted hunters from below the Mason-Dixon line. Looking at each other, they said, "Where the hell did all those nigger soldiers come from?"

WHO ARE THEY?

CHAPTER 2

GRAMPS

The elderly woman, still with wet hands from washing the morning breakfast dishes, sauntered out into the backyard, yelling as she often did in a still youthful voice, "He's on *Sky-Tech*."

An elderly man, hearing his wife, replied with a snide voice bordering on gruff, yet with a touch of humor. "Who? The President again?"

"In your dreams, buddy."

"Given this guy's record, it would be in my nightmares."

"Well, just in case your interested, your grandson wants to speak to you."

"Which one?"

"Seattle."

"Which one?"

"Garvey."

"Why didn't you say so?"

"I just did."

The elderly man leaped from his outdoor patio chair in slow motion, checked to see if his pants belt was tight and his zipper closed, then satisfied that the basics were in order, scampered with all deliberate speed into the house. An Olympian he was not. He headed for the "family room," where the latest *Apple Sky-Tech* connection was located. Half television, half what was once called a telephone, half computer, half household assistant, the AST was the latest electronic wizard "you've got to have" on the market. And apparently, according to his wife, they had to have it.

The elderly man was rather proud that both limbs functioned reasonably well. Though about to celebrate his 90-birthday, he had, at least until now, avoided titanium crutches, a damn walker, or an unwieldy wheel chair. How he detested the thought of being dependent on one of those ungainly contraptions. Except for a cane that he used to ward off amorous nurses in his doctor's office, or life insurance salespersons at his front door, he could pretty well navigate on his own. He took joy in that. The last thing he wanted was to be helpless, unable even to scramble about even in his own house. Now and then he did bump into something, which always led to the same response. "Who the hell put that table there?" Or, as he liked to say after almost tripping, "My wife's shoes will kill me one of these days." Of course, he refrained from such declarations when the shoes belonged to him. Nor did he ever make a remark when he banged into a wall due to his own imbalance. He did have his limits.

He also took great pride in the fact, that, given certain restrictions, he could still drive his ancient Navy-blue PT Cruiser in his immediate neighborhood as long as he didn't hit a toddler, the post person, or his spouse of 60-years. So far he had avoided these mishaps and kept a clean record with the DMV. That he cheated a bit on his eye test was, of course, was well known within the family, but fortunately now with the Automobile Club.

Inside the family room he picked up the *Sky-Tech* cell phone, brushed back long strands of silvery hair with a bit of spit with a strong right hand before voice-activating the senior-friendly device. As he did, he murmured to himself, "Still got enough hair to cover the old noggin." Then, remarking to no one in particular, he quoted an old family mantra, "Bald! Yuck!"

He was growing older. He knew that. Indeed, how could he not? The birthdays just kept piling up, along with his increased use of his Medicare benefits and visits to Urgent Care facilities. Getting older didn't bother him. He just didn't like thinking of himself as old. He preferred "elderly." The difference was slight, but important to him. Old meant "OLD!" Yuck! Elderly simply meant getting older. Sort of like good wine... Given a choice, he preferred the vino.

Seated in his favorite, well-worn black leather rocker, he eyed the numerous family pictures on the walls of the room. Most were old, dating back to when his children, Rachel and Matthew, were kids. He recalled sending negatives through the snail-mail to some firm, now defunct as the dinosaurs, that enlarged the pictures, 2-feet by 3-feet or more. The pictures were returned in a carton tube weeks later. He always looked forward to pulling out the pictures, now poster-size, and unrolling them. His wife, Jan, then took over. She adhered the picture to a stiff backing material, added hooks, and the picture was ready for hanging. The pictures were a constant joy for him. He loved seeing them each day. They connected the past to the present and were precursors, he hoped, of the future. Much like a glob of good glue, the larger-than-life photos kept everything reasonably together, family, the good times, and the happiest moments. In a world of conflict and change that was okay with the old guy.

He liked that. He realized, of course, that older folks seemed to indulge in such antics, eyeing the past as if everything had happened yesterday. Again, that was okay with him. The past was a constant companion, a welcomed buddy who had traveled with him through almost nine decades. Yet, truth be told, lurking in him was a still unsatisfied spirit of adventure too long denied. When he was honest about it, he secretly desired some spurring of the senses, some experience out of the norm challenging his life of predictability and repetitiveness that would carry him beyond the backyard chores and the local YMCA gym. A good mystery, he thought, would be just what the doctor ordered if it provided momentary escapism.

And truth be told, the elderly man, though not nefarious, was given to deviousness when necessary. This being the case, he was about to hatch a long awaited plot to have one more bite of the apple. That is, to hit the road and indulge a latent fantasy in one last adventure. Oh, how he wanted that. And this anticipated call from Seattle, he hoped, would set in motion his long delayed plan to pay back the debt, to honor a self-imposed obligation to the past, to make things right. That was important to him. He didn't want to die before a promise was kept.

He gathered his thoughts. He focused on one particular photo, his sixteen-year old plus grandson, Garvey. The boy was, as the elderly man liked to say, his favorite Washington State grandson in high school. This helped him draw a distinction with his other favorite grandson, Kieran, who lived in Los Angeles and was eight years older and attending UCLA. Intended to do graduate work there. Rounding out the cast was still another boy who competed for his affection was, Harlan, three years younger than his brother, Garvey. He was a favorite too. Along with Garvey and Kieran, he too had a photo on the wall. The boys were his pride and joy, "the apples of his eye." He loved to look at their pictures. Grandfathers tend to think this way. Not to be forgotten, however, was the special joy of his heart, Harlan's twin sister, Miss Wells, as he liked to call her. What a beauty. Try as he might, that one could really get under his skin with a shy smile and sparkling eyes. Turned him to jelly every time.

But getting back to Garvey. He was a stud. A big kid, two inches above 6 feet, 180 pounds, and solid. He was good looking. No question about that. With blazing dark eyes, and curly coal-black hair on chiseled facial features suggesting a generic inheritance of Black and white parents he might pass as someone from a some South Pacific island paradise. He, of course, elicited numerous romantic pangs of the heart from the distaff s side at Wilson High School. He was a scholar in the classroom with a near 4-point grade point average. He was also a fine athlete. Even as a freshman, he had made the varsity baseball team with high hopes of making the starting lineup in time. Apparently, he took after his father's baseball past, but not as a pitcher. Garvey would be a catcher.

And naturally, as his grandfather, the elderly man, lacking all pretense of objectivity, considered his grandson one the most terrific young man in his age bracket in the northwest. He was, when talking about the boy, given to joyous hyperbole.

And the kid was the key to the plot about to be hatched.

He turned to his wife, as he always did when technology was the subject, asking, "Is the system on?"

"You need to ask?" she muttered. "It's always on when family members call. The computer system recognizes their voices. Everything is automatic."

"No need to get huffy about it."

"Just reminding you."

"Lower the decibels."

"You're hopeless."

The old man really did know how *Sky Tech* worked. Unbeknownst to his wife he had secretly read the manual, even went to a couple of workshops rather than meeting with his cronies to discuss "what the hell was wrong with Washington?" He played dumb to get a rise out of his wife, whom he loved dearly, but still enjoyed teasing. The new *Sky Tech-4000* was the latest, most advanced system on the market. Once connected to a caller, he could see the person on the razor thin 80-inch television portal, which took up almost a whole wall. At the other end of the "cloud line," the caller could see him in vivid color and real time. On more than one occasion he had fantasized that a bewitching damsel, who had just emerged from the shower, had called him by mistake. Of course, he kept this possibility to himself. No need to disturb marital bliss, he figured.

"Garvey, how good to hear from you."

"Just checking up on you, Gramps."

Kids... The things they call their grandparents. With Kieran, it was "Grandpa." With Garvey, it was "Gramps." With Harlan, it was "Grand Pappy." And, of course, his only granddaughter, also got into the act. She referred to him as "Grand Pop." A rose by any other name is still a rose the old man thought with a sly wink to William Shakespeare.

"Wanted to make sure you got the sweater, Gramps. Your early birthday present."

"Nice sweater. Great color."

"You going to wear it?"

"Garvey, such a question."

Sweaters... They were a point of contention in the family. For years, he had refused to give up his tired, well-worn, dark-blue sweater. At Christmas and on birthdays, almost like clockwork, he could count on receiving a new sweater with the sender's hope that the old one would be discarded. The new sweater would be accepted nicely, tried on to show some semblance of gratitude, and then, when no one was looking, neatly hung up in the closet with the multitude of previously gifted sweaters. One more sweater, he reckoned, and he could go into the outlet business. Amazon beware...

"Well?

"Persistent, aren't you?"

Why the resistance? To some extent he was just being hard headed, obstinate, a senior citizen happily stuck in his old ways. Most family members bought into this explanation. Just a cranky old guy enjoying feuding with others... Another view, very much in the minority, suggested he simply liked the old sweater. As he liked to say, "It fitted him like an old glove." To some, he made the argument in a slightly different manner. "Why change horses in the middle of the stream?" He got that line from President Lincoln. What that had to do with sweaters was never explained. Still, the old blue sweater was like an old friend. He could probably take it into the next world if such a thing was possible.

"Thinking about wearing it today. The temperature really dropped today. Some big storm from Canada pouncing on us."

"Send me a picture."

"Do I detect skepticism?"

"Previous experience. Anyway, how's Grandma?"

"Beat the cancer scare. Healthy as a horse... Make that a Kentucky Derby winner. Betting on her reaching the century mark. It must be the German in her."

"What about the Irish in you?"

"Good for ninety-nine years, I'm told."

"By whom?"

"A little guy dressed in green, if you must know. Anyway, she sends her love. Still quilting, big time... Belongs to two book clubs these days. Tuesdays for 'murder stories.' Thursday for 'high drama.' And she's still reading three books to my one. She won't use the latest *Kindle*. Tried to buy her one. Got on her hind legs. Refused me flat out. Likes to actually hold the book, turn the pages, and place it on the nightstand. And before you ask, she's baking those chocolate chip cookies you like so much. Should be in the mail this week."

"Gramps, you there?"

"If you can see me, Garvey, I must be."

"How are you really feeling?"

"Okay for an older guy with two stints in his body, and a few other medical miracles. Not bad at all... Starting to feel like *Captain America*."

"Who?"

"Before your time."

"That's what you always say."

"Well, it's true, isn't it?"

"I guess so..."

"How's the household? Does your father like being a superintendent?"

"When the school board isn't on his case."

"Comes with the territory, and the big bucks. And Blair?"

"Mom is running three clinics for her new company, *Beat Depression Now*."

"Are they still rattling your cage?"

"Not really once we get past the homework issue."

"Don't sweat it. It's a generational thing. I bugged your Dad. He bugs you. Guess what happens next?"

"I bug my kids."

"Yeah. Spoken to your cousin, Kieran, lately?"

The two boys were more like brothers than relatives. Admittedly, Kieran was older than Garvey in the relationship. Eight years can make a big difference. So he was the big brother, as Garvey was to Harlan. Over the years they had spent considerable time together having California fun surfing off Malibu or snowboarding near Mt. Baker near Seattle. With their *Apple Zip-Phones*, they kept in touch notwithstanding the 1,000 miles separating them. Naturally, they talked about the things young men were intensely interested in, sports, girls, school, dating, dealing with parents, and other things better left unmentioned. In short, they were great buddies.

"Just last night."

"And?"

"Finishing up his Masters at UCLA in June. Cool, isn't it? Wants to go to grad school to become a history teacher like you."

"Tried to talk him out of it."

"I bet. Like you talked my dad out of teaching. And your daughter, my aunt, Rachel."

"They wouldn't listen to me."

"Not the way I heard it."

"Oh, yeah! How do you know?"

"Grandma. "

"I should have known."

"Gramps, can we talk seriously for a minute?"

"Why not? I'm on the *Senior Citizen Unlimited Plan*."

"You got my letter?"

"Kieran, you call an electronic 'Apple-cloud E-mail' a letter? A letter is something written on paper! With a postage stamp."

"Please, Gramps, I need your assistance. Dad said I should talk to you. Mom agreed."

"Okay. No need to bring in the big guns. What's on your mind?"

"I've read the volume you wrote for me and Kieran, and the twins, Harlan and Wells. You know, *US History, 1945 – 1960*. Really enjoyed the stories."

"Leading with flattery. Good strategy. That makes an older guy's day. But that isn't why you called, is it?"

"I need a topic for my AP US History class."

"Research paper?"

"Yes."

"Figures."

"More precisely, I need a topic related to race relations."

"Lots of possibilities."

"I need something unique, not the usual stuff, Reverend King, or Rosa Parks. Like I said in my letter, Gramps."

"You checked your mail recently, Garvey?"

"Got your letter in my hands. But I don't understand your answer. You didn't enclose a note, just those things: three coins and an old piece of cloth. I don't get it."

It was true. He hadn't written anything. He just taped three old coins to a blank sheet of paper and added the so-called "piece of cloth." No word of explanation, just two extra first-class stamps to cover his weighty response to his grandson. Snail mail, the last dying tradition of a senior citizen… However, given Garvey's digital-plea, his response was, he thought, perfectly appropriate. And very devious, he knew. No doubt about that. He wanted the kid asking questions. The idea had come to him as he read Garvey's electronic letter days earlier.

––––––––––––

Dear Gramps,

I know how you detest texting, long E-mails, everything but the written word. But I needed to reach you fast. I'm running out of time.

Kieran told me that you often suggested interesting topics to him when he was assigned term papers in history, both in high school and college. "Off the wall topics," was the way he put it. Really cool... Very special... You know something the other students might not doing ... I'm hoping you can help me. This research paper is worth 30% of my final grade. I need a good grade. But first I need something I can get my teeth into, something that will really motivate me. I seemed to be bored by many of my classes. Please make some suggestions. Remember it must be about race in America.

Thanks in advance.
Garvey,

———————

The elderly man watched the *Sky-Tech* screen. He could see Garvey. The kid looked worried. He was too serious for one so young. Okay to be that way on the baseball field. That was important stuff. Or with the cute girl in the back row in English. But for a history assignment... That was a waste of emotions.

He had decided to help Garvey. The kid was his grandson. But deep down there was another motivation, one that flirted with his advancing years, and tempted whatever time he had left. Altruism was not completely the focus here. A stream of selfishness ran deeply. Not the usual ego stuff, or some sort of greedy materialism. Rather, an adventure, perhaps a last one on the open road, was at the heart of the matter tied to settling scores with the past.

He could see the boy looking at the envelope. Slowly, Garvey opened it and took out three coins. He carefully placed them on the coffee table before him. He then peered into space, a quizzical look on his face.

"Those are special coins, Garvey."
"Never seen any like these before."
"Not surprised. They're pretty much out of circulation now."

"How do they relate to a topic?"

Good question the elderly man thought. Now could he provide an enticing answer to initiate the quest?

"Didn't I enclose something else?"
"Just an old patch. I think that's what it is."
"Not just any old patch, Garvey. It's alive with history."
"This patch?"
"And the coins?"
"They're tied to a topic?"
"Why else would I send them to you?"
"You're being elusive?"
"To peak your interest."
"Okay, I'm peaked. Now what?"
"We talk about Buffalos."

CHAPTER 3

AIRBORNE

"Okay, Gramps, I have the patch in front of me and the coins. Can you see them?"

"Clear as a bell. Let's start with the patch. What do you see?"

"An old patch."

"Fine. You're very observant. You'll make a great private eye. Come on, what do you see when you look closely at it?"

Garvey withheld his answer. He knew his grandfather was putting him through some sort of test. Always did when he asked him about things. He never gave a simple answer. Clarity was always lacking. This, he knew, was done on purpose. There was always a little slight of hand, a little deception to keep things honest. His grandfather liked to turn everything into a mystery.

Garvey looked hard at the patch, trying to see every last aspect of it: numbers, words, and pictures. But try as he might, he couldn't locate one buffalo. But that made no sense. Hadn't Gramps said, "We'll talk about buffalos?"

THE FAMOUS PATCH

"I see the word *Airborne,* yellow letters against a black background."

"Suggesting what?"

"The air force?"

"Close. What else do you see?"

""There's a white-colored parachute?"

"Suggesting what, Garvey?"

"When you jump out of an airplane, it helps to have one on the way down."

"Ah, a comedian. Now connect *Airborne* with a parachute. Logically, what do you get?"

"Paratroopers?"

"Question or statement?"

"Statement, Gramps."

"Excellent. Now what else do you see?"

"Golden rattlesnakes, peering up at a black tiger."

"Interesting imagination, Garvey. What you're looking at, my young friend, are wings, which the paratroopers earn once they finish their training. Cherished by all who jump."

"And the tiger?"

"Panther, ready to pounce on the enemy, Garvey."

"Really?"

"What about the numbers?"

"I see three fives. The numeral five written three times."

"Remind you of anything?"

"Fifteen… 3 X 5 = 15."

"Excellent computation, Garvey, but not the answer we're looking for."

"A number between 4 and 6?"

"Still with the jokes?"

Gramps was right, Garvey thought. I was being a smart ass with the old guy. Perhaps it was nervousness. The research paper was important to me. I needed a topic and Gramps, knowing this, seemed to be toying with me.. Suddenly and uncomfortably, he remembered one of his father's favorite lines. "Why don't we send donkeys to college?" Answer: "Who likes a smart ass?"

"Sorry, Gramps. Let me take another stab at it."

"I'm all-ears."

"A lethal paratrooper group, perhaps numbered *555*, has earned its wings, and is now ready for airborne duty. How's that?"

"Pretty good so far."

"The panther symbolizes the group, all tough guys, who will leap out of a plane, parachute to the ground, and then kick the enemy where it hurts most."

"Very good."

"But what does this have to do with buffalos?"

"Hold your horses, or in this case, buffalos. All will be made clear after we talk about *Miss Liberty*.

"Not the coins?"

"The coins exactly."

Garvey knew better than to duel with his grandfather. No way to jump ahead. The buffalos would have to wait. Some pretty girl was taking precedent. Apparently, Gramps was enjoying this protracted explanation.

"Fire away, Gramps."

"Can you see the picture I'm holding up?"

"It looks like a coin."

"Remarkable observation. What about this picture?"

"Another coin, or maybe the backside of the first picture."

"Very astute. These pictures are of the famous *Liberty Head* nickel, sometimes referred to as the *V-nickel* because of the 'V' on the reverse side. It was a five-cent coin first struck for circulation in 1883. It was last minted in 1913. The art work was done by Charles Barber, the Chief Engraver of the US Mint."

THE LIBERTY HEAD NICKEL

"This is important because?"

"Just indulge an old guy? This coin was needed to replace the original copper-nickel five-cent piece, the so-called *Shield* nickel. Lots of production problems with that copper nickel. A replacement coin was needed. There was a large commercial demand for a new coin, especially with the advent of coin-operated machines, which were fast becoming popular. Barber's design for the coin had the classic head of Liberty. On the reverse side he engraved the Roman numeral for 5 to designate the denomination of the coin. Of course, lots of people, caught up in the fervor of the recent war with Spain, thought the 'V' stood for victory. Flushed with victory over Madrid and the recipient of new territories, Cuba, the Philippines, and Puerto Rico, it was a natural misunderstanding. Creating an empire can do that."

"Imperialism."

"Or, Garvey, as President McKinley suggested, 'manifest destiny,' departing our shores for the Pacific. Now, getting back to the coin. Around the number a wreath was placed. It was composed of wheat, cotton, and corn. A full recognition of America's agriculture and the bounty we raise to feed the world."

"Nice."

"Nice. That's all you have to say, Garvey?"

"Very nice?"

"Better. Now a cool fact, a bit of trivia."

Gramps was sidestepping. Garvey recognized the ploy. The right hand was talking. But the action was in the left hand. But, as always, why?

The US Mint, Garvey, was supposed to stop making the coin in 1913. However, five coins were surreptitiously struck. No one knew how this happened. Lots of uncertainty here... The five coins remained in circulation. Today they are one of the most expensive coins in the world. Rich collectors bid for them. The last known coin to be sold openly was in 2010. An anonymous collector paid a measly $3,737,500. Not bad for a nickel."

"Freaky."

"Freaky? That's the best you can do?"

"Very freaky?"

"Very funny. For your penance, I'll tell you about buffalos. Isn't that what you've been waiting for?"

"Finally."

"Between the years 1907 to 1909, the US Congress made the decision to beautify America's coinage. The US Mint was instructed to do so. An engraver, James Earle Fraser, was given the task of replacing the *Liberty Head* nickel. This was in 1911 during the administration of President William Howard Taft. One restriction was placed on the engraver. The coin had to celebrate America's history, especially the American West.

"Why that?"

"Lots of reasons. The one I like is this: the country was still infatuated with the frontier, covered wagons rolling toward the Oregon Territory, the Indian Wars, and the sprawling legends almost as large as the West itself."

"As you said, lots of choices. But why, Fraser?"

"Fraser was an interesting choice. Born in Minnesota in 1876 he saw the closing of the American frontier and heard stories of the injustices done to the Native-Americans, who were pushed onto reservations. After graduating from the Art Institute of Chicago, those stories and his creative talents as a sculptor led to many works celebrating these subjected people. He tried to carve into stone something of their life. Had a real sensitivity for their history."

"Sounds like a cool dude."

"Cool indeed. Fraser poured himself into the task. His eventual designs impressed the President, a bison, the buffalo by any other name, and an Indian, a native-American. In 1912 Fraser's designs were approved. In 1913 the first nickel would be struck and the US Mint would continue making this 5-cent piece until 1938."

"This is the buffalo you were talking about?"

"Sort of, but let's mention a few things first about the descendent of the wooly mammoth. Was he not the subject of lore and legend, whether in the journals of Lewis and Clark or the sharp shooting of Buffalo Bill Cody? Was not the buffalo the supermarket of its day, a COSTCO on the hoof or a Wal-Mart, and so important to the plains Indians? Did not this creature provide food, furry clothing, and bones for tools? The buffalo was the indispensible animal. Beavers were nice for hats. Elk and deer provided necessary meat. But only the buffalo operated a full-service establishment."

"You're sounding like a commercial, Gramps."

"I'll ignore that comment. As for the Indian, the original native-America, Fraser's image was, don't you think, the iconic profile of the fearless warrior found in Hollywood's version of the Old West? "

"You want me to write about a coin? What does this have to do with race relations in our country?"

"At the moment, nothing. But just wait, my grandson of little patience. For a moment look at the coins I sent you."

"I've never seen nickels like these."

"I'm sure you haven't. They were only produced between 1913 and 1938. They had too many manufacturing problems. Eventually they would be discontinued."

THE BUFFALO HEAD NICKEL

Garvey knew his grandfather was setting him up. Still, there was little he could do but play along. At least there was a buffalo at the end of the tunnel.

"Okay, Gramps, what were the problems?"

"Smart boy. Check out this picture I'm holding up. It illustrates the three main problems with this particular coin."

"First, because the buffalo and the Indian face were raised, they were struck indistinctly at times. Second, they tended to wear faster than other coins and previous nickels. Third, once in circulation, the date was worn away too quickly. For these reasons, it was decided to mint a new nickel in 1938."

Garvey could smell a rat. Why 1938, he asked himself? Why not earlier? If there was a problem, why wait 25-years? Gramps was teasing and testing again.

"The new coin, the *Jefferson* nickel with which you are familiar, I believe, was designed by Felix Schlag. It would replace the 'buffalo nickel.' I wonder why the Mint waited until 1938? Any ideas?"

"Was some law involved? Was Congressional approval needed? Was there a waiting period?"

"Right and right again and again. By law, a coin can only be replaced after 25-years of service, and Congressional approval is a requirement. And that's how the *Jefferson* nickel came about. Nice looking rendering of our third President, don't you think? On the reverse side was his home, Monticello in Virginia. Not many residences can make that claim, at least on a US coin."

JEFFERSON NICKEL

"Your home would be nice, Gramps. You know, the common man, the average guy, a middle class fellow."

"Perish the thought. Coins commemorate the few, not the many."

"Seems undemocratic."

"Back to the Jefferson coin you social radical."

Here it comes, thought Garvey. Gramps is leading to something. I know it. He's got that look on his face. What's he up to?"

"Garvey, got a Jefferson nickel? If so, pull it out and check out Jefferson's home, then compare it to the picture I'm holding up."

This is it, Garvey reflected. I can feel the question coming some difference between the coins, my coin and his picture. That's got to be it. But what is the difference?"

"See any difference between your coin and the one in the picture I've got."

"Just one."

"Oh?"

"There's a 'P' above Monticello in your picture, but not on my coin."

1943-P Silver Jefferson Nickel

"P" Mintmark: Philadelphia Mint

"Direct hit, young man. Now why do you think the 'P' is there? I'll give you a hint. It was only there between 1941 and 1945."

"It had to do with the war years, I think, perhaps World War II. Maybe the Mint used a different metal because of wartime needs. "

"Garvey, you have the makings of a good detective. The 'P' letter designated a 'war nickel' that was only part silver."

"It's nice to get one right now and then."

"Okay. Feeling pretty smart, aren't you? Ready for a little more trivia? Try this question on for size. Who is the Indian on the buffalo nickel? If stumped, just make the throat-slitting gesture."

Garvey complied. What could he do? No way he would know the answer. Gramps was in the driver's seat again. That being the case, he flattened his hand and then moved it quickly from left to right across his throat. Self-slitting was not to his liking, but what's a kid in need to do? Out there somewhere was a research paper topic. And maybe closer than he thought ...

"James Earle Fraser needed a face, Garvey. The engraver, you'll recall. Remember? He checked out old newspapers. The Library of Congress provided many photos. He investigated art museums. Talked to folks on the reservations. Eventually, he had lots of photographs to work from, different Indian faces from all over the country. Check out these pictures I'm holding up. That's what an authentic Indian should look like: strong, dignified, a great fighter, a powerful medicine man, and a wise counselor to his people."

"Gramps, I get the picture. How did he decide?"

"These are pictures of the Indian Fraser eventually focused on, a Oglala Lakota Chief by the name of *Iron Tail*, who had been a star performer in Buffalo Bill's Wild West Show. Indeed, he was an international personality, who had appeared in Paris at the Champs-Elysees. He had also entertained in Rome and London. Wherever he went, the aristocracy couldn't get enough of him. For Fraser, however, it was the face, the profile that attracted the engraver, not the celebrity status of the Indian. This was the face Fraser wanted on the new nickel."

CHIEF IRON TAIL

"There's a story behind every story with you Gramps."

"That's what makes history so much fun, Garvey, the story behind the story. For example, the likeness of *Iron Tail* doesn't end with the nickel. In 2001 the American *Buffalo Silver Dollar* was issued by the US Mint to commemorate the opening of the National Museum of the American Indian in Washington, at the Smithsonian Institution. Once more the Chief's profile regaled our money, as did the almost forgotten buffalo on the reverse side. To help the Smithsonian, a surcharge of $10 was charged for each minted dollar. The profits went to the museum. Collectors lined up to buy the coin. This is proof, I think, that money makes money."

"And my research topic?"

"Be a detective, Garvey. What do we have as evidence, so to speak? A patch. Three buffalo nickels. So what's the connection? How does a paratrooper's patch relate to a buffalo nickel? How does a five-cent coin tie in to three fives on the patch? As is the usual case, the answer is right in front of our nose. Our historical nose, that is."

"I guess my nose is too large. It's covering up the answer."

"Then a little history lesson is needed."

———————————

"Back in 1943 during World War II, the Army, urged by the White House, created a new Army battalion at Fort Benning in Georgia. The battalion was made up of voluntary transfers from other Army groups. What was the importance of this? On the surface, apparently nothing... New battalions were being formed each day. The demands of a global war required this. But this battalion was only made up of Blacks, who until this moment, hadn't really been permitted to fight in the war with other American soldiers at the front. That is in combat roles. America's army, though fighting the racist dogma and practices of the Nazi regime, was at the time segregated, discriminatory, and racist. The causes of this situation were deeply rooted in our history and paid no homage to the Blacks who fought in the Civil War for the Union, or others who stormed San Juan Hill in Cuba, Nor did it acknowledge those who fought to put down the bloody insurrection in the Philippines, or the role of blacks in the First World War, especially the famous all-Negro brigand from Harlem.

The White House wanted to end this, as did Negro newspapers, politicians, and millions of Negroes related to former slaves. Pressure was put on the War Department. The problem could not be ignored. A decision was made to implement a Black combat unit.

The newly created battalion was designated the 555th, and would become the only Black-American parachute unit in the Army during World War II. The officers and men wanted a nickname. They chose the 'Triple Nickles' for themselves. They used the original English spelling for the word. They wanted their name, not just their color, to distinguish them from others. The 555th was also drawn to the "buffalo nickel." The likeness of the buffalo reminded the men of another time, the post-Civil War period when another group, former slaves, and freedmen from the North, rode the Great Plains fighting America's Indian Wars. We refer to these earlier men as Buffalo Soldiers. In making this connection, the 555th battalion fused the past and the present, Black soldiers on horseback and paratroopers in the sky, united across time and space."

THE BUFFALO SOLDIERS

"Making sense to you now, Garvey?"

"A nickel with a buffalo on it?

"Not to put too fine a point on it, yes."

"The 555th parachute unit... Three fives... Three nickels... Now written 'nickles ...'"

"And?"

"A nickel with a buffalo on it. The Buffalo Soldiers... Combat soldiers... All related to the 555th."

The elderly man was proud of his grandson. He had connected the dots and disclosed the history embedded in the past. All was going according to plan.

"Here's the deal, Garvey. You want an unusual topic. Something special others don't even know about, including quite possibly your teacher, right?"

"Right, Gramps."

"Then consider researching the 555th."

"Some Black guys in the Army?"

"Not just some guys. A special group of men, who kicked in some doors."

"Gramps, what are you talking about? What doors?"

"Garvey, you live in a world not of your making. You are the direct beneficiary of what others did to make your world."

"I don't understand."

"Understandable. Let me be more direct. You come from a mixed family. Your mother's father, your grandfather, Gartha, was a Black man. Her mother, your grandmother, Theresa, was white. On your dad's side his parents were white. You are the result of DNA enjoying a wild ride through the intermarriage of whites and Blacks. This DNA circus-car ride will probably continue when you marry some day, especially if she is a dark-haired Hispanic beauty, or a lovely Asian woman. Anyway, you yourself are partially Black, partially white, and whatever is in between. For some, that makes you an African-American; that is Black, a person of color and a minority."

"Okay, I get that. Dad has explained some of this to me. Mom, too."

"But has he told you about the 555th's story? About their struggle to fight for equality and fairness for Black people while also fighting the Nazis? Has he, or anyone, told you the honors they earned during the war, even as they served in a segregated Army and experienced discrimination wherever they were stationed in America? Has he even told you about your name, Garvey?"

"About my name, yes. Marcus Garvey; he was interested in helping former slaves return to Africa. I know about him. But not the 555th beyond what you have said."

"Then it's time. Research the 555th. But a word of caution, Garvey; if you take on this subject, you're going to learn many disconcerting things about America that aren't brought up in school, things that might prove politically incorrect to some, even less than patriotic to others. But if you can handle it, you'll be a stronger person, and most importantly, you'll realize how fortunate you are that others paved the way in the fierce arena of civil rights and race relations, even during wartime. Before Martin Luther King there were young men leaping into an empty sky, proving that they were good soldiers and entitled to social justice. Again, because of their sacrifices, you enjoy the benefits resulting from kicking in the doors of prejudice and bigotry."

"Pretty heavy duty stuff."

"And are you up to it?"

"I want to be. But where do I start?"

"Find out about a fellow called Jim Crow."

CHAPTER 4

THE MAN WHO JUMPED

<u>TEN DAYS LATER</u>

"He duped me."
"What are you talking about, Garvey?"
"He fooled me, Mom."
"Who?"
"He's nefarious."
"Nice SAT word, son, but I'm still puzzled as to who did what?
"Gramps, that's who, Dad!"

Garvey was in the kitchen with his mother, Blair, and his dad, Matthew The young man was excited, perplexed, and beside himself, but that hardly explained his demeanor and barely accounted for his distress. What was troubling him went somewhat beyond that. It could, however, be explained away quite simply. He had been had, he would claim, by Gramps, big time.

"And just how were you duped?" his mother asked.
"Six days… For six days I chased a mirage. In the library, on the Universal Global Internet, everywhere I looked for a shadow. "
"Thank you, Garvey, for clearing up my question."
"Does this help, Mom. Gramps set me up!"
"Again, meaning exactly what?"

Garvey and his parents were sitting at their large rectangular-shaped dinner table in what would best be described as a vast room with no walls between the kitchen, the dining room and the living room. Just one large open space, a perfect venue, one might conclude, for venting voluminous tirades against a charming manipulator, who had conned an innocent grandchild. At least, that's the way Garvey saw it. Seated as they were in this beautiful room, they had, if they turned their heads a bit to the right or left an amazing westward–looking panoramic view of Seattle's busy seaport. They could see the great container ships from all over the globe carrying within their larger-than--life crates the consumer goods of the world, all the merchandise that found its way onto the Target and Sears shelves, not to mention Wal-Mart and COSTO. As for the other ships, especially those from Japan and Korea ... The Hondas, Toyotas, and Kia cars drifted across the Pacific, neatly stacked, bow to stern, many levels deep into the ship's bowels. And from their perch they could also see the immense cranes lifting the containers to waiting railroad flatbeds, or onto trucks by the hundreds, all a part of the complex transportation system that linked Tokyo to Seattle. This they could see and, if they listened hard enough, they could hear the words of Carl Sandberg, America's poet of the bustling, striving, and clamoring business world of Chicago: the stockyards, the blast furnaces, the smooth, marble banking houses, and the bigger-than-life granaries. Of course, Sandberg could have also been speaking of Portland, Seattle, or San Francisco.

Hog Butcher for the World,
Tool Maker, Stacker of Wheat,
Player with Railroads and the Nation's Freight Handler;
Stormy, husky, brawling,
City of Big Shoulders...

And from their rooftop, had they been so inclined to go outside, a different vista awaited them. They would have seen Mt. Rainer, a commanding, hopefully still dormant volcano, glistening in the sun with a new mantle of powder-white snow. Contrasted with this were the rings of evergreen forests, towering trees reaching to the very heavens, and bursting with the lumber to build millions of homes. Not quite Eden, but certainly a sight to behold.

In the warmth of their home still brimming with the smells of newly baked sour dough biscuits and now devoured scrambled eggs, Garvey and his parents should have been at peace with the world. The eggs, layered with Swiss cheese, tiny chunks of honey-baked ham, and a sprinkling of finely cut chives, were Garvey's favorite Saturday morning breakfast. Add to that hot apple cider and his world should have been beyond compare. But, given Garvey's emotional fussing, and verbal fuming, that was, of course, not the case.

"Gramps, Mom. He tricked me!"

"You have made that abundantly clear, Garvey."

"He told me to research a fellow named Jim Crow. He said it was the best place to begin my research of the 555th Airborne."

"So?"

"I spent the whole week looking for a person who doesn't exist."

"You told him?"

"Yesterday. And you know what his response was? 'What took you so long to figure it out?' Not, 'I'm sorry.' No contrition. Adding salt to the wound, he said, 'but I'm sure you did find out a great deal about Thomas Dartmouth Rice, didn't you?'"

"Who's he?" his father asked, a blank stare on his face.

"Yes, who's that?" Garvey's mother questioned, an equally nonplus look on her face.

Garvey glanced sharply at his mother. Like her, he had an almost bronze-color to his skin. And like her his eyes were coal-black, as was his hair. Their facial features were finely cut giving them a startling presence that demanded the attention of others. They were, of course, as noted earlier, a mix of black and white genes, mixed not once, but twice through the heavenly randomness of DNA. For all intense and purposes, they might have just stepped off a Polynesian island, splendid Tahitians. Still slim and very attractive, Blair was a beautiful woman. Garvey knew this to be true. After all, that was the way his father described her, calling her a "stunner." And his dad, Garvey knew, was almost always right.

"Mom... Dad... Rice was the father of Jim Crow."
"The person who never existed?" they responded in unison.
"Exactly. Rice was a real person. Jim Crow was Rice's invention."

Blair gave Garvey her best teacher look, the one which arrested unwanted, unworthy behavior, that chilled a student's heart and froze the individual in place, heart pounding, that said in an unstated manner, "Kid, would you like to live to your next birthday?" The "look" was reserved for those special moments when exasperation prevailed over infinite patience and prudence, suggesting in those moments that no parent or teacher should be in the possession of a firearm. It was a look that Garvey rarely saw but readily understood.

"Garvey, you have less than one minute to explain this mystery! The clock is ticking."
"I think you should heed your mother's injunction, Garvey," his father added sympathetically. "No need for the Harlan and Wells to see blood on the floor. Your brother and sister are very sensitive," he added with a smile. "I guess that's the way it is with twins."

Garvey got the picture.

"We need to delve into the past, long before the Civil War."
"Well, then, I'll have another cup of coffee, Garvey. Onward into the past, and an answer."

"Thomas Dartmouth Rice was a traveling actor, a performer on the stage, first in lonely frontier theaters, later in the big cities of the 1830's, and ultimately in London and Paris. He was described as 'talented, tall, and wiry.' During his travels, especially in the South, he observed and absorbed the traditional song and dance of plantation slaves, African-Americans in today's parlance, or Negroes as they were called in the post-Civil War days. Or again as Blacks if you prefer. This is an equal opportunity group. A born mimic, Rice quickly captured the essence of local speech and gestures. Soon he could impersonate a Negro slave in voice, language, walk, everything but color. You could say he had a God-given aptitude for this and an appetite for stage fame. It was this gift that would make him a small fortune and provided a slightly larger fame. In time he would be known as 'Daddy Jim Crow.'

"Legend has it that supposedly Rice once saw an elderly black stableman, perhaps in St. Louis, or New Orleans, possibly even Vicksburg. No one knows for sure. Anyway, this stableman had a crooked leg and deformed shoulder. If this unsubstantiated story is true, the old man was singing about Jim Crow, and punctuating each stanza with a little jump. The man was dressed in rags with a battered hat and torn shoes. Apparently, Rice created his "Jim Crow" character based on this old Black man." This apparently innocent decision was to have widespread social consequences beyond anything Rice might have anticipated."

"Garvey, you're saying there was no actual Jim Crow."

"Right, Dad. Just Rice."

RICE AND HIS CREATION

"Just a caricature?"

"An exaggerated form of one."

"That being the case, enlighten us."

"Sort of like a man who was never there," Blair added.

"What, Mom?"

"Nothing really. Just a figure of speech."

"Rice opened up his own theater in New York, the Park Theater, where he blackened his face and introduced his Jim Crow minstrel act, an old stableman on stage, dressed in rags with a battered hat and a crooked leg. Then in a stilted voice emulating in accent the old man's intonations, he sang his Jim Crow song, beginning with this line, *'Turn about and wheel about, and do just so. And every time I turn about I Jump Jim Crow.'* It was from a song Rice had written and entitled, *'I Turn About and Wheel About.'* At each performance, he added a stanza, always keeping the song new for his repeat audience. The song, the new verses, and his mimicking caught on with the public."

Some of the most commonly quoted lyrics included:

Come, listen all you gals and boys. Ise just from tuckyhoe;
I'm goin, to sing a little song, My name's Jim Crow.

CHORUS (after every verse)
Weel about and turn about and do jis so,
Eb'ry time I weel about I jump Jim Crow.

I went down to the river, I didn't mean to stay;
But dere I see so many gals, I couldn't get away.

And arter I been dere awhile, I tought I push my boat;
But I tumbled in de river, and I find myself afloat.

I git upon a flat boat, I cotch de Uncle Sam;
Den I went to see de place where dey kill'd de Pakerham.

And den I go to Orleans, an feel so full of flight;

Dey put me in de calaboose, an keep me dere all night.

When I got out I hit a man, his name I now forgot;
But dere was noting left of him 'cept a little grease spot.

And oder day I hit a man, de man was mighty fat;
I hit so hard I nockt him in to an old cockt hat.
I whipt my weight in wildcats, I eat an alligator;
I drunk de Mississippy p! O! I'm de very creature.

I sit upon a hornet's nest, I dance upon my head;
I tie a wiper round my neck an, den I go to bed.

"Rice created Jim Crow with these lyrics?"

"Mom, yes he did. No social media in those days. Just word of mouth brought in patrons. And in the newspapers of his day, they promoted his act. His version of the old Black man took on a life of its own. The way Rice acted out his portrayal of the old man characterized the way most whites thought of Negroes before the Civil War, and especially in the former Confederacy after Appomattox."

"Hard to believe" his father added.

"Led to the legacy."

"Meaning what, Garvey?" his mother quickly asked.

"The Jim Crow character on stage was applauded for, and gained acceptance because, it was common in the 1830's to see Negroes mocked as 'uneducated and irrational.' At its worst, these stereotypes saw Jim Crow as savage, primitive, and dangerous. A potential Nat Turner dancing on stage. Better to belittle him than to have him rise in rebellion against the whip. Rice's description of a slave, even a Northern free Negro, reinforced a negative stereotype of Negroes. Audiences saw what they wanted to believe."

"Did Rice begin his show with this in mind?"

"He was a product of his time, Mom, no better or worse than other people. His views were typical of his day. Whether it was his intent to cast dispersion on Blacks, well that's difficult to know. That he wanted to attain notoriety as an actor, there's no question about that. Unfortunately, his characterization of Jim Crow took hold and was extended to all Black people with negative connotations. The stage caricature of a Negro person became reality for many Americans. Same thing happened with Hollywood's portrayal of indigenous people, referring to them as savages on the frontier, bloodthirsty killers of innocent folks heading westward. Ultimately, and so unfairly, Jim Crow would be code for an entire overt caste system of social discrimination practiced in the South, but not limited to southern states."

"You seemed to have learned a great deal, Garvey. But one thing, why do we still use the term, Jim Crow?"

"Good question, Mom. After the Civil War and during the Reconstruction Period in the South, beginning in and around 1870, segregation laws were instituted in the former states of the Confederacy. The memory of Jim Crow, the stage character, was simply transferred from the theater to the legislatures of the Deep South and the racially inspired laws passed. I don't believe Rice ever foresaw this. It was an unintended consequence of what he did on the stage. In any event, the segregationist practices instituted by the reemergence of Southern whites to political power opened the door to a form of American apartheid and Jim Crow just walked through the door. Jim Crowism ruled the day."

"Perhaps Gramps did you a favor, Garvey."

"How's that, Dad?"

"He gave you a mystery to solve. And you did. In a kind of backward way, he motivated you to get into the research. Maybe you're being too harsh on him."

"You're taking his side?"

"Just asking you to consider another view."

"He's that devious?"

"Wouldn't put it past him."

"Maybe I need a second opinion."

"Possibly. Up to you. In the meantime, we'd like to know more about the Jim Crow laws Gramps wanted you to research."

"He said I'd learn a lot of ugly things about America."

"Did you?"

CHAPTER 5

JIM CROW

Garvey considered his mother's question. Had he? The simple answer was yes. Gramps had warned him. He had asked him if he was up to it? Naturally he had said yes. No way would he suggest otherwise. No historical yellow streak ran down his back. He was a tough guy when it came to looking under the carpet of America's racial history. At least that's what he had told himself. Nevertheless, once he saw what was there, he realized how unprepared he really was. What he saw was, as Gramps had said, ugly.

"Jim Crow laws were state and local laws in the United States enacted mainly between 1876 and 1965. Stated this way they sound so innocent. Just laws, ordinances, judicial decisions, nothing more... In essence they mandated de jure racial segregation in all public facilities in Southern states that composed the former Confederacy. By government edict and law, the races were to be separated in every possible way. Racial segregation, how bad can it be? Sounds so innocent until you looked at what it meant in the real world. Whites and Blacks would be segregated in public schools, public transportation, restrooms, restaurants, theaters and drinking fountains. And that was just the beginning. The separation of races in daily life led to social conditions for the former slaves that were inferior to those provided for whites. Within the social fabric of economic life, educational possibilities, and social interaction, Blacks were put at a disadvantage. They were second-class citizens.

"All this was done purposely and consciously, as one group, using its political power and controlling the police and judicial power, systematically oppressed another group. Politically, conservative white voters in the South joined the southern wing of the Democratic Party for the sole purpose of maintaining a system of racial separation, creating in the process what came to be called the "Solid South," essentially a one party political system below the Mason-Dixon line focusing on Southern Democrats. And, if this wasn't enough, the nation's Supreme Court justified and rationalized the inherent inequalities of racial segregation based on the notion of "separate but equal status for the races," That came about in the infamous 1890 Plessy vs. Ferguson decision. Half the notion was true. The races were separated, but they were not equal."

Garvey stopped. He needed to catch his breath. He also needed to control the anger boiling up in him, and, if truth be told, the tears that threatened to flow, cascading down his youthful face, a sort of historical anguish that came about in his confrontation with "ugliness." He stood up, walked to the large picture window, and peered out at the beauty of Mount Rainer, still covered with snow. So innocent and clean, he thought. So different from what he now knew.

"Garvey, you okay?"
"Working on it, Dad."

Parents, believe it or not, can be cool. Garvey's parents rose to the occasion. They didn't ask him what the "it" was. They simple waited for their son to continue. In a few minutes he did, sitting down again and speaking in a strong voice obviously filled with emotion.

"The system of Jim Crow laws depended on disenfranchising the 'Black voter,' who had been protected in Southern States by federal troops following General Robert E. Lee's surrender to General Grant in 1865. Beginning about 1872, Jim Crow laws were passed in the South by white legislatures with three specific goals: first, remove all freely elected Black politicians from office. Second, end Black voter participation through a system of poll taxes, literacy tests, residency requirements, and voting record-keeping procedures. Third, create a myth portraying the Black as primitive, illiterate, and incompetent --- an individual incapable of holding public office, even to participate in free elections. As a consequence, this meant even the most illiterate and impoverished white person could vote, but not an educated and prosperous Black. That this was a contradiction did not, however, get in the way of Jumping Jim Crow. By 1896, Black voters were almost completely eliminated from voter rolls, and certainly from political office in the South."

"Terrible, Garvey, writing people out of history."

"Gramps warned me, Dad."

"But how did they do it?"

"By controlling the government, the police, and the local courts. By manipulating the system to the advantage of whites at the expense of Blacks."

"Examples, Garvey?"

"You won't like them, Mom. Many of the methods employed used violence to control, if not intimidate the freedmen: murders, people lynched, homes burned down, churches destroyed, and potential voters beaten. Heavy fines levied. Jail sentences handed out. And this was in addition to the non-violence obstructions put in the path of Blacks who wanted to vote."

"You're right. I don't like it."

"South Carolina had the first literacy test, the notorious 'eight-box' ballot. It was adopted in 1882. The test was quite simple. Voters had to put ballots for separate offices in separate ballot boxes. There was a voting box for the governor. There was another voting box for a seat in the state legislature. All these boxes were meant to confuse the Black voter. And on and on it went. A ballot put in the wrong box was thrown out. But to get the ballot in the right box, a degree of literacy was needed. In short, you had to read what was on the ballot and the box. This was at a time when 40 to 60% of former slaves were illiterate compared to 8 to 18% for mainly poor whites. In order to rig the system even more, the boxes were constantly shuffled and reshuffled. By law, no literate poll worker could assist illiterate voters by arranging their ballots in the correct order. The sole purpose was to, of course, reduce, if not eliminate, the Black vote."

"How unfair, Garvey."

"It get worse, Mom. Another aspect of the literacy test was the 'satisfaction test.' This was put into place to placate illiterate white voters who wanted to vote. Potential voters, both Black and white, had to read a portion of the Constitution or some other legal document. It was up to the poll worker to determine if the passage had been read appropriately, or if the voter had an understanding of the passage. In order to protect even the most illiterate white voter, the 'grandfather test' was also used. This permitted white voters who did not pass the literacy test to still vote if they were descended from someone eligible to vote in 1867 the year before Blacks received, by federal law, the right to vote. That was the Fifteenth Amendment."

"I didn't realize…"

"You didn't know about this, Mom?"

"Of course, I did, at least, a little. How awful to live under those conditions."

"You didn't learn about this in high school? College?"

"Hardly anything."

"Dad?"

"Me neither."

" Of course, I heard stories, Garvey. But nothing like this."

"No! It gets even worse."

Blair glanced intently at her son. Perhaps for the first time, she realized her boy was turning into a man. Not just physically… That was all too apparent. It was his intellect, she thought. He's bright. He's college material, no doubt about that. But he's also a sensitive soul. She wondered how all this research would affect him? True, she and his dad had discussed a few issues related to race with him, but not this stuff. Truth be told, they preferred to leave these black pages hidden away in the dustbins of history. They were much too painful to discuss. Yet, here was their son dusting away these cobwebs, forcing the family to confront an appalling past. He was treading where, she realized, she was reluctant to go. As was her husband...

THE STRUGGE TO VOTE

"This system of rigid anti-Black laws became a way of life in the South that maintained a cardinal belief that whites were superior to Blacks. Therefore, whites had the God-given right to rule over an inferior people. Based on this view Backs were relegated to the status of second-class citizens. That was their place in life. A caste system was ordained. Christian ministers, for example, justified the system, teaching that whites were the 'chosen people,' that Blacks were cursed to be servants. In other words, God supported racial inequality. That other men of the cloth, reading the same *Bible,* reached different conclusions, did not trouble most Southerners. The "scriptures" meant what you said they meant."

"Much like the US Constitution, Garvey."

"How's that, Dad?"

"It means exactly what the last Supreme Court decision upholds."

"But decisions can be reversed?"

"True. They can also be avoided, stymied, even disobeyed."

"Like the Fifteenth Amendment?"

"Precisely. The Constitution provided for the vote, but states had to implement the law and that did not always occur. Am I right, Garvey?"

"Pro-segregationist politicians, using fear as a motivator, harped on the dangers of integration and the 'mongrelization of the white race,' which would destroy the white race through sexual unions. Sex, so to speak, was off-limits between a white woman and a Black. No intimacy was permitted. Of course, in the dark of the night little was said about a white man forcing his attentions on a Black woman. In the first case, a Black man could lose his life for crossing the sexual line. In the latter case, well that was, of course, different."

"Mixing the races by force?"

"Exactly, mom."

"Ugly."

"It gets worse. Newspaper and magazine writers, and, of course, later radio narrators constantly referred to Blacks as niggers, coons, and darkies in an attempt to reinforce Black stereotypes. The propaganda was insistent, constant, and unconstrained. In this manner of speaking, the Black, by using these terms, was dehumanized. He was no longer a person. He was a "thing." True, he had legs, arms, and a heart. Certainly, he could walk, talk, and breathe. And, yes he could think. He could reason and function. He could do things. But he could not escape his fate to be an oppressed human being in the South and to a lesser degree in the North."

"As you said, Garvey..."

"If this wasn't enough, many believed that violence was necessary to keep Blacks at the bottom of the racial hierarchy, whether by the government, groups, or individuals. This was no idle threat. Violence, both real and threatened, undergirded the Jim Crow laws. By example, if a Black tried to vote, he risked losing his job, having his house burned to the ground, or even being killed. On a daily basis, whites could physically beat Blacks with impunity with the victim having little legal recourse because the Jim Crow legal system was all white, the police, prosecutors, the judges, and juries. The system, as always, was rigged.

"The most extreme form of violence used to maintain social control in the South was lynching. For that we are indebted, historically speaking, to the KKK and other extra-legal organizations that took the law into their own hands in the post-Civil War decades."

"Do we have to get into this, Garvey? Lynching people, I mean."

"Ugly stuff, Mom. The worst, just as Gramps said it was. It was hard for me to handle what I learned. Our US History text doesn't even mention lynching of Blacks. Nor did my teacher. Can you believe that? It was like these hangings never happened."

"You're handling it?"

"Trying."

Blair found herself at odds with herself. Her teen-age son, a quiet boy living in in an affluent neighborhood of Seattle, had somehow found a way to deal with the repugnant, painful subjects, which she wanted to avoid. Where had one so young found the courage to look evil in the eye? Gramps had set something in motion, which, it appeared, had to be played out. That old man, she thought, not the elderly guy he liked to be called, had deliberately steered her son into a historical morass of discrimination and humiliation that she had spent a lifetime avoiding, overcoming, ignoring, at least in an historical sense. While Garvey's dad did not always agree with her, he did quietly support her. He was always responsive to her sensitivities.

What was Gramps up to, she thought? Certainly, researching the 555th Airborne was a great topic. But why descend so far into the past? For her, she knew, the present was safer. True, she reflected, living in Washington and California had excluded her from the worst prejudice against Blacks, but not everything. Coming from a mixed family did not provide immunity from inane comments and racial stupidity. Now, here was her lovely son, on Gramps' cue, dredging up the past, reminding her that, be her a professional or not, there were those who still harbored racial animosity. But, what could she do? She could ask Garvey to get another topic. But how would she justify that? No, that wouldn't work. Truly, there was no choice. Where her son went she would have to follow. As would her husband… In support of their son they would be a team.

"Okay, Garvey, let's hear it."
"Mom, you're sure?"
"No."
"The statistics are appalling. Between 1882 and 1968, there were 4,730 known blacks lynched in the South and adjacent border-states. Known killings must be emphasized. No one knows how many went unreported. No one knows how many people were shot, burned to death, beaten to death But of the 4,730, 3,440 people were Black, mainly men. No accurate statistics were kept before 1883. Therefore, no one really knows how many people were lynched before that year. A lynching tended to be a function of mob actions, or, if you will, extra-legal murder, sometimes carried out in the most sadistic manner. Victims were hanged, or shot. Others were burned at the stake. Some were castrated, dismembered, or simply beaten to death. Law officials simply looked the other way.

"And what was the purpose of all this. Clearly, to keep blacks in their subordinate place through what might be called a neo-colonial policy based on violence. Install fear. Maintain the fear. This was especially true in small and middle-sized towns where many whites resented any economic competition from an 'uppity" former slave.' In such mainly rural towns somewhat off the main road, the glare of a large city newspaper or local government was less existent. Atrocities were possible."
"Garvey, please."
"Just one example, mom."
"Only one."
"Two photographs from the past highlight this barbarism. One photograph I came across was taken on January 15, 1889, about 139 years ago. George Meadows was lynched in Jefferson County, Alabama for looking at a white woman, or so the mob claimed. Another photo I found was of Laura Nelson, a mother who tried to protect her son from

a mob. Both she and her son were accused of shooting a local sheriff. The mob was unwilling to await a court trial.

GEORGE MEADOWS AND LAURA NELSON

"Violence was always in the background. And always the same issue was paramount to Southern white governments. How to you keep the Negro subordinate? By fear, by intimidation, and by extra-legal actions, but always though the threat of violence. On an ordinary day when whites and Blacks had to work together in the Deep South, how do you maintain racially oppressive norms in a civilized society short of the rope? By constantly enforcing a Jim Crow etiquette and procedures in every aspect of daily life backed up the law. For example,

1. A Black male could not offer a handshake to a white person because it implied being socially equal.
2. Blacks and whites could not eat together unless the whites were served first and some sort of partition was placed between them.
3. Blacks were introduced to whites, never whites to Blacks.
4. White motorists had the right-of-way at all intersections.

5. Never curse a white person.
6. Separate drinking fountains for the races.
7. 7. Never demonstrate superior knowledge to a white.
8. No colored barber shall serve as a barber to white girls or woman (Georgia).
9. Colored persons could not be buried in white areas of a cemetery. (Mississippi).
10. Separate waiting rooms shall exist in public bus stations. There must be separate ticket windows in such stations. (Alabama).
11. Wine and beer cannot be sold to whites and Blacks within the same room. (North Carolina).
12. Public libraries shall have separate reading rooms for the races.
13. No Black person can have custodial control over a white person. (South Carolina).
14. White and colored militia troops shall be separated with Black soldiers under white officers. (North Carolina).
15. Colored and white inmates shall have separate apartments for both eating and sleeping (Mississippi).
16. No co-mingling in a theater
17. No integrated neighborhoods.

"Taken as a whole, these varied efforts to maintain rigid control over the emancipated slave and his descendants were called Black Codes and were built on pre-Civil War laws and statutes, which totally regulated what Black people could do. Blacks could not, for example, assemble, bear arms, become literate, speak freely, or testify against a white person. To one degree or another, the post-Civil War period continued this effort. The intent was to restrict the freedom of a whole class of people on the basis of race. That is, to continue white supremacy even if the country had adopted the Thirteenth Amendment (ending slavery), the Fourteenth Amendment (defining citizenship) and the Fifteenth Amending (right to vote). Southern whites viewed these amendments as forced on them by General Grant's cannons, and not of their own volition. They viewed the new societal arrangements as a 'corruption of race and gender relations that historically favored white males.' Given this view, the Black Codes were a logical consequence of whites clinging to political and economic power."

"Garvey, I can't believe you researched all of this."

"Not just this, Mom. Much more…"

"It's not too much?"

"The research?"

"No. What you're learning…"

"The ugly, you mean?'

"Yes."

Garvey just shrugged. What else could he do? Screaming at the past wouldn't change anything. Pretending nothing happened was understandable, but childish. What was couldn't be erased. Gramps had pushed him into something. All he could do was move on, which meant in this case, delving into the past.

Blair, as did her husband, felt immense pride in her son. He had taken on a repugnant topic and was dealing with it. She wondered what he felt. After all, he was from a mixed family. That made him a Black, a child of an oppressed people, at least in a historical sense. Did he feel anger? Hatred? Frustration? He had to be feeling something. So far he had not expressed any outrage. But he was also part white. How did he feel about that? Half of him had oppressed the other half at least metaphorically. So far the sharing had been on an intellectual basis, not an emotional one. Was her son keeping his feelings bottled up? If yes, would they flood to the surface at some point? Then what? To learn about the 555th Airborne was one thing. To learn about these horrid things --- the Black Codes --- that was quite another thing. She wondered what his dad was really thinking?

Garvey's dad was a realist. No "wish" spectacles colored his view of the past. What was, he believed, was. What could or would be was up to us. He lived in the now, but not uninfluenced by the past. Just not controlled by it. That was his hope for his son. Indeed, for all his children.

"Mom, I can handle it. Don't worry."

"Mothers worry."

"Gramps was right."

"He was?"

"It's like Dad always says, "Before you can paint the room, you have to spend time preparing the room."

"I don't…"

"I've been cleaning the historical room. Out there somewhere is the 555th, but first I have to clean the room. Does that make sense?

"I suppose so."

"There's still more cleaning, Mom."

"You've been talking to your grandfather? Still listening to him? Still angry at him?"

"Both, mom. But like you said, maybe he did me a favor. Pushed me hard. Made me poke my head into that sordid past we've discussed. Probably wouldn't have done it on my own. Venting has helped me. I got a few things off my chest."

"More than a few things, I think."

"So what happened to him?"

"Who, Dad?"

"Rice."

"Dad, he made a lot of money for his time. And he liked people to know he was well off. Wore expensive clothes. Costly rings. His popularity peaked in the years 1832 to 1844. He portrayed his 'Negro act' before sold-out houses, both here and in London. He popularized what was called 'blackface entertainment.' He also performed in more than 100 plays."

"He was popular!"

"Know anything about his final years, Garvey?"

"Just a little, Dad. He died on September 19, 1860 in New York. Apparently, he died from some sort of paralysis that affected his speech and physical movements. There is a view that his death was alcohol related. That does go along with the view that he died a pauper having squandered away his wealth in saloons. Public funds paid for his burial. He was interred at the Green-Wood Cemetery in Brooklyn, New York:

plot: section 47, lot 13088. He was fifty-two years old at death. Might visit his gravesite someday."

"What?"

"You know, Mom, share a few thoughts. Who knows, he might even answer me."

"Garvey…"

"He's only kidding, honey."

"Not completely, Dad. Gramps thinks we should have a conversation with the historically deceased now and then. Said if was good for the human spirit."

"You believe that?"

"Gramps might have a point. Trying to keep an open mind."

"So what now?" Garvey's dad asked.

"Gramps dropped another clue."

"I should have known."

"1872. I need to check out that year. Then it's on to New Orleans. Apparently, I have an appointment there. Historically speaking, of course."

"And that has what to do with Black paratroopers?"

"I haven't the faintest, Dad."

CHAPTER 6

DISPUTED ELECTION RETURNS

<u>A FEW DAYS LATER</u>

As opposed to the earlier kitchen brawl Garvey was now feeling quite good about himself. His angst was gone. Had he been wearing a slightly tighter shirt his expanding chest of self-satisfaction would have popped all the buttons. A zipper would have untracked and flown into low earth orbit. To be fair this was not just an unchecked ego, coated in hubris, and on a hedonistic kick. No, Garvey really deserved the sustained applause swirling around in his mind. He had done it. He had cracked Gramps' latest cue. The year 1876 was no longer a mystery to him. He knew why the year was important to the 555th Airborne and to the entire odious system of Jumping Jim Crow discrimination and segregation that took root in the former Confederacy and elsewhere. As to New Orleans, well that particular clue still needed to be figured out. But for now, Garvey, as noted, was on a deserved high. That his grandfather had not put another one over him he found very satisfying. He recalled a recent conversation with youthful glee.

"Gramps, I did it."
"Wonderful."
"I can explain the mystery."
"You met a beautiful woman? You understand women?"
"Not that."

"Well, don't worry, you're entering the vulnerable age. You'll soon be dealing with these questions."

"Gramps, I worked it out, at least one of your hints, I know what you were getting at."

"Which one?"

"1876."

"I'm impressed."

"So am I."

"I can expect something."

"Check your computer."

Garvey was sitting in the "mans' cave." That's what his dad called it, a place for manly moments, but open, as it had to be, to the ladies. It was a large room under the house, what some would call a basement. It was furnished and finished, and for Garvey his special world. It was in this room where he had taken his first tentative steps at nine months. He knew that as a fact. His childhood had been recorded. Seemingly, hundreds of digital photographs taken by his parents attested to this, including motion pictures, by-product of digital phones. They also had pictures of him chasing the family cats, never quite catching them, but for no fault of trying. It was in this room that he discovered the wonders of electric plugs and hot wires connecting all sorts of electronic equipment. And here he had heard the oft-used word, "No." In this room he had also wrestled with his dad, first as a toddler, later as a boy, and then as a teen. Again, miles of video "takes" certified that he had won two out of three matches thanks to a gracious father with a compassionate heart. It was in this room that he watched innumerable football games with the family, cheering on the University of Washington team and the Seattle Seahawks, not to mention the Mariners. How many hot dogs and plates of beans had been devoured in this room? How many beers and soft drinks had been drunk? And how many bowls of popcorn had toppled over when impassioned fans leaped to their feet after a Huskie "TD?" More than one, that was for sure.

Garvey's bedroom was conveniently adjacent to the "mans' cave." It, too, was a large room with a hide-a-way Murphy bed with two large mattresses. Getting into bed was like scaling Mount Everest. One misstep and you were on the floor. A large window gave the room an airy feeling and a delightful view of the terraced backyard. Just outside of the room was the family spa. He had spent considerable time in the spa with his parents, splashing, laughing, and loitering beyond the reach of "this must be done now." A door in his room gave Garvey quick access to this watery world and its willful "timeout."

In his room was a desk at which he had spent uncounted hours doing homework at the incessant prompting of his parents. It was also where he spent time with his stamp collection. Gramps had interested him in this neat hobby a few years ago. There was something fascinating about the stories stamps told, the history they encompassed, or the personalities they depicted. One could lose oneself, as Garvey often did, in this world of tiny illustrated moments of history. Needless-to-say, it was at this desk where he worked on his research of the 555th Airborne and prepared his latest extended E-mails to crusty-old Gramps.

"Tuesday, November 7, 1876... Keep that date in mind, Gramps. That was the cue you gave me. It was almost too easy once I got into it, believe it or not? Figured it out in no time. A new president was being elected that day. Or should I say two presidents were possibly elected that day? By evening, the election results, spurred by the click-click of telegraph keys, informed the country of its new leader. The whole country waited with baited breath in what was understood to be a close race, even though both political parties claimed an edge that would get them into the White House.

"At first I was caught off guard by my own research. How was it possible to have two presidential candidates elected on the same day? A schizoid candidate, wasn't that a possibility? And what was the 'edge' each political party was claiming? In time the answers came clear to me.

"On election day, the country waited for the results. One most interested and an astute observer of all things political was Daniel Sickles, a Republican, who, after attending the theater on election night, decided to stop by Republican headquarters to see how badly the party was doing. Sickles, though mostly unknown in history, was a colorful, former congressman with four notable accomplishments. First, he had been acquitted in 1859 for killing his wife's lover, who just happened to be Philip Barton Key, the son of Francis Scott Key, the author of the *Star Spangled Banner*. The shooting took place in Lafayette Square across the street from the White House. Second, his acquittal was based on the first known use of the insanity plea. Sickles claimed he had been driven insane because of his wife's affair. The judge and jury bought it. Third, he had lost a leg at the Battle of Gettysburg in 1863 and, surviving this, went on to become a Union general, wooden stub and all. He also claimed that he was the hero of the battle, not fussy, old General George C. Meade. After the South's defeat, he argued this position in newspapers for years. He was not one to give up easily. Fourth, he was appointed to serve as America's minister to Spain by the Grant Administration in 1869. He served until 1873. Apparently, he had done this job well. No one was shot in Madrid and he kept his other leg out of harm's way.

SICKLES

"Sickles was about to add another chapter to his fascinating life. This time it would lead to the most serious constitutional crisis in America's political history, at least before the resignation of President Richard Nixon in the 1970's.

"At Republican headquarters on that November 7th, Sickles learned the dismal truth. The Republicans were losing. When the final tabulations were eventually made public, the Republicans nominee, Rutherford B. Hayes, had 47.9% of the popular vote or 4,034,142 folks on his side. The apparent winner would be Samuel J. Tilden, the Democrat, with 50.9% of votes cast, or 4,286,808 votes. Hayes was behind almost 250,000 votes in the popular vote. It looked like the Democrats were back in power."

"You're hedging, Garvey. What do you mean it looked like the Democrats had won?"

"As if you didn't know. Gramps."

"Tell me."

"As Sickles scanned the disappointing results the proverbial light went on in his mind."

"Illuminate me."

"He perceived a way to a Republican victory where no one else did. He was pure calculating genius at work."

"You're stalling."

"I'm creating dramatic tension."

"Garvey…"

"Sickles wasn't overly concerned about the raw vote. That is, the popular vote. He was interested the Electoral College count. That's what made you president. Each state's total count was based on its two Senators (2 electors), and its members in the House, who were based on population, and could, therefore, vary with each state. The larger the state's population, the greater the electoral count. The winner of the popular vote won a state's electoral vote. It was a winner take-all business.

"Obviously, under the right conditions, it was quite possible to lose the popular vote, yet win the election if a candidate secured the necessary electoral count. This, of course, was what appealed to Sickle. But was it possible?

"Tilden had 184 electoral voters. Hayes had 165. Tilden was one electoral vote shy of the necessary 185 to be President of the United States. Hayes, however, needed 20 more electors if he were to be elected. As Sickles digested the results, a slight smile crept over his face one would have to believe. Three states with Republican partisan governors, Florida, Louisiana, and South Carolina, had disputed results. And in Oregon, there was a question concerning one elector. In total, there were 20 electors up for grabs. If the disputed electors went to Hayes, he would win with exactly 185 electors. Of course, that was a big if.

"Sickles was determined to make the improbable possible. He would make a fact out of an 'if.' It was the battle of Gettysburg again for him, but this time political maneuvering and deal making in cigar-filled rooms would substitute for cannon and Union soldiers braced for action at Cemetery Ridge.

"Sickles immediately sent telegrams to each governor in a disputed state, telling all of them to 'hold the line.' This was code for 'don't certify a Democratic victory.' And more to the point: 'only certify Hayes as the winner in your state.' The partisan governors understood and responded accordingly.

"Sickles telegrams threw the country into a constitutional crisis, which almost erupted into a second Civil War. Before the crisis was resolved, each state in question would submit two sets of election returns with each political party claiming victory. Who would be President? That was the question everyone asked for the next four, excruciating months. It wouldn't be answered until two days before the new president was to take office. Talk about cutting things close."

"Nicely set up, Garvey. Right on point."

"Where you wanted me to be?"

"Where I encouraged you to be."

"But still in the dark about all this, Gramps. What's the relationship between Sickles and the 555th Airborne 75-years later?"

"As if you didn't know. Come on. Make the connection."

"Really pushing, aren't you?"

"Didn't earn my crusty reputation being a pansy."

"A what?"

"Nothing. Before your time."

"You always say that."

"Talk to me."

"Once the Civil War was over in 1865 the main issue dividing the two major political parties were the questions of Reconstruction policy. That is, how would the warring, now conquered states of the Confederacy, be reunited under Old Glory? The Republican Party of Abraham Lincoln supported federal intervention in the former Confederate states in order to protect the newly freed slaves. This protection took many forms, including jobs, educational opportunities, and the right to vote, even the opportunity to be elected to political office. All of this, of course, meant that federal troops would be used to protect Republican governors, newly elected mainly with the Black vote, from the usurped white population unhappy with their aggrieved situation. Succinctly, the defeated Confederacy would be treated as just that, a government that lost the war.

"In short, the South would have to be militarily occupied indefinitely. That, of course, ran counter to the American experience. Americans don't like to be under the foot of soldiers. And nothing is indefinite in our history. Change is the norm, not permanency. Consequently, the zeal to save the union and to free the slave had run its course by 1876. Crusades, no matter how justified, are hard to maintain. The nation was ready to turn a historical corner.

"Military force had been necessary to protect the numerous socially idealistic teachers, mainly Northern women, and God-fearing clergymen from hostile Southern whites. In other words until life was normalized the former slave needed the protection of federal troops. The great fear in the North was that reentering Southern states under white rule, regardless of the Civil War amendments, would replace the plantation, slave system by putting freemen in a near servitude caste, where basic civil liberties would be absent and economic oppression the rule of the day.

"There was ample proof of this. White-dominated Southern legislatures elected immediately after the war but before Blacks could vote, passed laws regulating the working conditions and pay of the newly freed slaves that, in effect, made them little more than poorly paid wage-slaves with no visible chains. These laws anticipated the stringent racial discrimination and segregationist practices of Jim Crow laws on steroids, which would take root in the South after 1876.

"As an aside, it is well to remember that every member of the 555th Airborne, who grew up in the South, and experienced racial discrimination tied to 'Jumping Jim Crow.' Their lives would be forever colored by the unfolding events of 1876. These paratroopers were not immune to what Sickles had set in motion.

"The first restored Southern state governments did exactly this, giving rise to Radical Republicans in Congress who effectively disbanded these white-empowered legislatures. Military districts replaced the civilian authorities in which Southern whites were essentially stripped of their political rights. In a large measure they were being treated as a conquered, occupied people. Given this, Black voters, out numbering whites, elected, as expected, their benefactor, the Republican Party, to power.

"The Democratic Party was split on the issue of military occupation. Northern Democrats were sympathetic to the need for troops. On the other hand, Southern Democrats were vehemently opposed to such federal intervention by the Johnson and Grant administrations. The Southern wing of the Democratic Party wanted the complete removal of occupying federal troops. In time this was slowly done as more moderate white Southerners came to power, at least as far as they ratified their new state constitutions, which included the vital protections of the 13TH, 14th, and 15th Amendments. Again, emancipation, due process, and the right to vote... In response, the number of federal troops had dwindled from 15,000 in 1867 to 3,000 by 1875. By that year Southern whites had "redeemed,' or won back control of their state legislatures except for three states, Louisiana, Florida, and South Carolina, where the last federal troops were still an occupying force, and where the disputed electoral votes existed."

"Excellent summary to this point, Garvey. Now what?"

"Sickles understood the social calculus at work. Unhappy white citizens, disputed election returns, and the North exhausted by the war and its aftermath. Used carefully, these realities might turn a Republican defeat into a White House victory."

"And how would he do that?"

"That fraud was rampant in these three Southern states was never a question. Whites, acting as paramilitary groups aligned with Southern Democrats, intimidated Blacks with threats of violence to keep them from voting. Republican political meetings and rallies were disrupted. In other cases, more sophisticated techniques were used. Ballot boxes were stuffed with Democrat Party votes. Another avenue was to distribute to illiterate blacks voting materials for Tilden disguised with Republican symbols to get people to vote for the wrong party, if indeed they got to the polls. Again, with both parties claiming victory and the three states in question returning different returns, the question was what to do about it?"

CHAPTER 7

BACKROOM DEAL

"And what was done, Garvey?"

"Subterfuge, political connivance, and behind the scene chicanery."

"Perhaps you fill in the gaps?"

"Politics in its most rudimentary form."

"The presidential candidates, Tilden and Hayes, said little. They left it to others to challenge, criticize, and refute the accusations flying through the Washington D.C. air. Surrogates were everywhere on the stump. Given our contemporary presidential campaigns, it was still seen as unseemly for presidential candidates to campaign vigorously and passionately on behalf of their platform.

HAYES (R) TILDEN (D)

Both sided used mud-slinging to advance their favorite. Truth became the first casualty of the election. Facts were distorted. Smear campaigns were conducted. Fear was used to motivate voters, one way or the other. The candidates, on the other hand, tried to be above it all. That is, presidential... They tried, where possible, to campaign from the front porch by talking with reporters, who then took their views to the newspapers. Who were these two presidential candidates seeking the highest office in the land?

"Rutherford B. Hayes, the Republican candidate, was a "reforming" governor of Ohio, where he tried to replace the political patronage system with a professional civil service. It took seven ballots at the Republican convention to nominate him. He was 'a compromise' candidate. His biggest asset was that he was free from the taint of political corruption. He had, therefore, few enemies and only modest critics. In accepting his party's nomination, he stated clearly in writing that he would only serve for one term if elected. Hayes was a genuine hero. He had been wounded several times while serving in the Union Army.

"Samuel J. Tilden was the governor of New York. Like Hayes, he was known as a reformer. He had gained fame as New York's Attorney General when, though against great odds, he prosecuted and beat William Marcy "Boss" Tweed, the corrupt political boss of New York City. Tilden did not served in the Union Army. Naturally, this point was not lost on the Republicans, who constantly reminded voters of this, a tactic the Democrats called 'waving the bloody shirt.' As the Republicans repeatedly said, 'Not every Democrat was a rebel, but every rebel was a Democrat.' Naturally, this sort of rhetoric reinforced the view that smearing a candidate has a long and accepted place in American politics.

"On two issues, the candidates were in agreement. First, civil service reform was needed within the federal government. Patronage, which led to incompetency, was corrupting the government. Second, they agreed that Reconstruction should end. Both Northerners and Southerners were in concert with the candidates, though for different reasons.

Northerners were weary of the crusade to emancipate and protect the former slave. The Union had been saved. Slaves had been freed. The dead were buried. That was enough. Harsh economic reality, noticed in both the North and South, dictated that Blacks were competitors for jobs, and a slice of the American dream. And the pie was only so large. Enough had been done on their behalf. As for Southerners, they simply wanted to reestablish white-controlled governments unopposed by federal troops. If they had to live with the end of slavery, let it be so on their terms."

That was the background, Garvey thought. That's what he e-mailed to Gramps. The country was, it seemed to him in 1876, again approaching again the dreadful hours before Fort Sumter was fired upon. As he considered that thought, he glanced around him. Immediately, he saw his father's collection of photographs on one wall just above where he sat. His father referred to them as the "black and white" photos. There was a photo of Garvey's great-grandfather on his dad's side, Samuel Livingston, who had been in the Navy during both World Wars. Two other photos showed his great-uncles Vic and Walt Preston, who had also served in the Navy during World War II. Arranged on a shelf nearby were the medals belonging to the great-grandfather. One medal stood out, the Purple Heart. Since the time of George Washington this medal was always awarded to soldiers who were wounded in battle or killed. The medal had been presented for wounds sustained long ago in an almost forgotten naval battle off of the Philippines in 1944. On the shelf there was also an American flag sheltered in a triangular wooden casing. Gramps had been given it by the Veterans of Foreign Wars when his father, Samuel, died --- that and a smart military salute, a few words, and a *Bible.*

Garvey wondered how he would do in war? It was a question asked by young men from time to time. Would he have the courage to stand and fight? This was not a football game, where win or lose you went home after the contest. This was not about a video game where violence, no matter how authentic and realistic, was still the product of imaginative software and Hollywood magic. Digital characters died, not the one manipulating the joystick. No, war was something else. He had read too much about the great, but bloody Civil War battles, Gettysburg, Fredericksburg, Vicksburg. All were brutal battle waged with no quarter given. So many young men perishing for a cause, for the Union, and for "Old Virginia." For ideas invisible to the eye, yet powerful enough to send great armies into battle. And in 1876, was this not again almost the case? Isn't that, he reflected, what he told Gramps?

"Gramps, as the constitutional crisis deepened, tensions increased throughout the country."
"To be expected considering the issues."
"And you know what happened?"
"I did teach history, Garvey."
"But you won't divulge."
"That's your job."
"Challenging me, aren't you?"
"My M.O. at the moment."

"The most militant Democrats warned that a Tilden victory would mean 'blood on the streets.' A congressman from Kentucky, Henry Watterson, railed, 'a 100,000 men would march on Washington' if Tilden was not installed in the White House. Headlines in newspapers learning toward the Democrats blandished bold, blistering type across the front pages, *Tilden or War!*" The fever pitch of convulsing views caused General William Sherman to order four artillery companies to the nation's capital to maintain order. In the White House President Ulysses S. Grant put out a neutral statement that neither side endorsed, but ultimately would have to accept."

No man worthy of the office of President should be willing to hold it if counted in or placed there by fraud. Either party can afford to be disappointed in the result, but the country cannot afford to have the result tainted by the suspicion of illegal or false returns.

"Black Americans feared a Tilden victory would mean the reestablishment of slavery in the South, or something akin to it such as tenant farming. Already this practice, perhaps better called a form of involuntary servitude, was maintaining the old plantation system under near slave-like conditions. Already, the whites were resorting to violence to silence the Black vote. Already the promise of the three Civil War "amendments" was being called into question by the most partisan of white conservative Democrats.

"How to have a legitimate occupant of the White House, yet maintain peace in the country was now the primary question before the Congress? On January 10, 1877, just a few months before the new president would take office, a bill was introduced for the creation of a commission independent of Congress for 'the final adjudication of the disputed electoral returns.'"

"Why didn't Congress handle this hot potato, Garvey? Handing off the problem to an outside commission suggests a loss of nerve."

"Things weren't exactly as they seemed, Gramps. Independent of Congress might not mean exactly what it suggested."

"You'll explain."

"The bill called for an 'orderly, multi-institutional, bipartisan solution' to the crisis. Fifteen members would be on the commission. From the Senate, five senators (3 Republicans, 2 Democrats)... From the House, five representatives (three Democrats, 2 Republicans)... From the Supreme Court, five members (4 chosen on the basis of geographical diversity, who would then select a fifth... Since the Constitution did not spell out how such a crisis should be handled, the Congress was improvising on the go. With this in mind, President Grant signed the Electoral Commission Act on January 29, 1867.

"The commission ended up with 8 Republicans and 7 Democrats due to the Supreme Court justices, who nominated a fifth justice, who was an independent, but shifted to the Hayes's side. Regardless of the evidence provided the commission, a partisan vote would mean a Hayes victory. Tilden's supporters cried foul. Hayes' people rejoiced. And the country threatened to tear itself apart.

"The commission went forward with its work. Witnesses were called. Evidence was collected. Records were scrutinized. Each side made its case. The inquiry ended just two days before the inauguration of the next president. The final verdict was the expected 8 to 7 decision in favor of the Republicans. That was never in doubt given the heated partisanship of the day. Hayes was judged the winner. He received all 20 of the disputed electoral votes. Hayes would win, 185 to 184, Publically, the Democrats fumed. Privately, they were less impassioned and more conciliatory. The party would not challenge the decision. No 100,000 men, guns loaded, would take to the field. Peace would prevail.

"Of course, the question that comes to mind was why? The answer was not found in the hallowed halls of the Congress, nor in the marble home of the Supreme Court. Rather, the crisis was averted in a smoke-filled room in an old hotel in the nation's capital."

Garvey's thoughts were interrupted by Gramps.

"Kid, I have to hand it to you. You really nailed this part of the research."
"I got into it."
"You've got a thing for history."
"I needed to know what happened, Gramps."
"You've got the thirst, Garvey. Damn if you don't. You've sunk your teeth into the 555th. Like a bulldog, you'll hang on, twisting and turning until you know the whole story. Right?"
"You knew this would happen?"
"Suspected it, Garvey. Nothing more."
"I bet."
"Whatever, Garvey. Time for you to finish the story?"
"The part I like best, Gramps."

"The Wormley's Hotel was a five-story hotel at 1500 H Street, NW, Washington, D.C. The hotel was owned and operated by James Wormley He was a most interesting character in at least three ways. To begin with, he was a freeborn Black man. He had also spent time in Europe learning fine culinary skills. Lastly, according to him, he had been at the bedside of Abraham Lincoln when the president died. Perhaps a fourth note should be added. As the proprietor, it was his fate to host the behind-the-scene meetings, upon whose outcome rested the fate of the nation and the destiny of the entire Southern Black population.

"Representatives of each party hurried to his hotel to hammer out a deal all sides could live with. No one wanted an outbreak of violence. No one really wanted to upset the Hayes victory. Something had to be done. How ironic, of course, that the future of former slaves and freeborn Blacks should be discussed in a hotel run by a Negro. One could almost hear the irrepressible Thomas Dartmouth Rice adding new verses to his "Jumping Jim Crow" song.

"The Hayes and Tilden delegates realized that no legal mechanism alone would adequately resolve the crisis. There was no appropriate mechanism in the Constitution to remedy the situations. Also, passions were running too high. The country was a tinder- box just waiting for a careless match to light up the night. What such an explosion would mean was too difficult to predict, too awful to contemplate. Would Tilden's people actually take up arms? Would the Blacks respond violently to any white effort to reinstate the slave system? Would Congress split into warring groups? Would the rule of law fragment and collapse under the weight of partisan anger? What would the effect be on the economy? That is, what would happen to business and commerce, if not banking and Wall Street? All of these questions seemed too great for the elected mortal representatives of the people. It would be up to "interested parties," acceptable to both candidates, to reach a compromise through secret, backroom negotiations.

"Specifically, it got down to this from the Republican perch. What would it take for the South to accept a Hayes victory? Stated in another manner, what would it take for the Tilden Democrats to forgo victory? The two questions, actually reflective sides of each other, were at the heart of the matter.

Through sharp debate the answers came.

"First, Southern conservative Democrats wanted the remaining federal troops pulled out of Louisiana, South Carolina, and Florida. The military occupation would end. Doing this, of course, meant the end of 'reconstruction' in the South. It meant returning the South to its native sons. The implications were easily discerned. Ultimately, Black political participation would be reduced, if not eliminated. The Black vote would cease in the old Confederacy. Whites would regain control. The southern wing of the Democratic Party would replace Republican office holders.

"Seen from the perspective of the former slaves, it meant the end of federal troop protections and the probably erosion of their civil liberties. But not only this… Public and private schools staffed with teachers from the North might be discarded. A neophyte Black business class could die stillborn. The chance to create a flourishing middle class would evaporate. Central to these views were two realities in the "redeemed" states where federal troops would no longer protected the Black. First, the right to vote was at-risk. And second, intimidation and violence by extra-legal groups would be used to assure white supremacy. These realities were well known to all, Hayes and Tilden supporters alike.

"The Hayes' representatives agreed to remove the troops. Once he was sworn in, Hayes would make this a first order of business. History marks that he did. Second, Southern Democrats wanted at least one position in the cabinet. The region was tired of being locked out of decisions at the highest level. This was agreed to with little debate. The cabinet position tenured was Postmaster General. The individual acceptable to all sides was Democrat David Kay, a US Senator from Tennessee. Why Postmaster General? Certainly, the position had none of the fanfare of State, Treasury, or War. Two reasons explain all. Those cabinet positions would never be offered to any Democrat. But most importantly to Southern politicians, they were really unimportant in the larger scheme of things. What was important was patronage, the power to provide jobs and positions to loyal friends and/or those you wished to influence. No other cabinet position controlled more patronage than the Postmaster-General. In a sense, it all came down to a simple horse trade: Southerners wanted patronage. Republicans wanted the presidency.

"Third, the South, destroyed by the war, wanted to rebuild its industrial capacity. This began with railroads. Southern railroad interests wanted a transcontinental railroad through the South. It also wanted Northern investment. In short, the South wanted a latter day Marshall Plan to rebuild the region. Promises were made to do so. Investments were made to some degree during the Hayes Administration, but not in the continental railroad envisioned by its proponents.

"The agreements reached by-passed and superseded the usual congressional procedures by which business was conducted. The agreements, however, provided a solution to a problem unanticipated by the framers of the Constitution. The agreements became known as the Compromise of 1877. They cleared the way for a final and necessary resolution of the contested presidential election sufficient to overcome a threatened filibuster by Tilden supporters in the House during a boisterous session lasting from 10:00 a.m. on March 1st to 3:38 a.m. on March 2nd. At 4:10 a.m., the last of the disputed electoral votes were counted. As anticipated all 20 electors went to Hayes, who won a one-vote Electoral College majority, 185 to 184.

THE FINAL COUNT
1876 PRESIDENTIAL ELECTION

Candidate	Party	Popular Vote %		
Rutherford B. Hayes	Republican Party	4,034,142	47.9%	185
Samuel J. Tilden	Democratic Party	4,286,808	50.9%	184

"Hayes would be the next president. But the position came with a price. For many, he was reviled as 'Old 8 to 7.' Other referred to him as 'his fraudulency,' or 'Rutherfraud B. Hayes.' A good number Democrats hated him because they believed his party stole the election. With equal passion, many rank and file Republicans disliked him for removing the last federal troops from the South and the protections they afforded Blacks. Another view was kinder to Hayes, believing that he saved the country from another conflict of arms, that only a Republican could have ended Reconstruction without a significant backlash. That the issue of civil rights for the former slaves floundered and then largely disappeared from the agenda of both political parties until the mid-twentieth century. That was the price the Black population paid for national peace.

AN IMPERFECT COMPROMISE

"As for Tilden, he summed up his defeat, eloquently pointing out:

'I can retire to public life with the consciousness that I shall receive from posterity the credit of having been elected to the highest position in the gift of the people, without any of the cares and responsibilities of the office.

Many would argue Tilden stated the case truthfully and with a bit of historical humor thrown in for good measure.

"Thanks to the Thirteenth Amendment, slavery would never expand into the Western territories regardless of which party was in power. Tenant farming would emerge, but only economic bondage, not slavery. Thanks to the Compromise of 1877 there was a Union and not another civil war. The Old Confederacy --- in time with all Southern states "redeemed" --- would become the "Solid South," the bastion of conservative Democrats bent upon implementing and maintaining Jim Crow laws during most of the next 75 plus years.

THE PRICE BLACKS PAID

It was done, Garvey, thought. The election of 1876 was history. He understood it now and its relevance to later days. But, what of Gramps? Would he approve the research? For reasons he couldn't fully explain, Gramps' opinion meant a lot to him. It was no longer about just a school assignment. It was about the past and some invisible, almost mystical line connecting him to the 555th. And Gramps was the key to it all, prodding and pushing with his "cues," fastening him ever more tightly to these airborne troops of the 1940's. Having considered this, Garvey wondered what the next cue would be? Something to do with New Orleans... But what would it be?

All this Garvey shared with Gramps, including a few last thoughts about Sickles. The man who spotted the 20 ballots Hayes needed died on May 3, 1914. He was 94 years old. He was buried in Arlington National Cemetery with full honors. For his heroism at Gettysburg he was awarded the Congressional Medal of Honor. All that was a few days ago. Since then not a whimper from Gramps... Then, precisely at that moment, as if on cue, the phone rang. Staring at Garvey on the telephonic television screen was Gramps with a big smile on his face. In his hand he held Garvey's research, gripping the papers securely.

"Garvey, I am so pleased. You did it. You've got the heart of a sleuth, slithering through the past, figuring out what happened."
"Slithering?"
"Sleuthing."
"Okay, Gramps. Got another clue? Something in New Orleans?"
"A whole basket."
"One would be nice."
"If you insist: 163 US 537"

CHAPTER 8

PROFESSOR RICHMOND'S TEST

"Dad, you're not coming in?"

"Big meeting today, Garvey. Can't break it. Anyway, you'll be fine. Professor Josiah Richmond knows you're coming. And he's delighted."

"And why is that?"

"Simple. It's not often a high school student is interested in the professor's personal research."

"He's been researching the 555th?"

"Lifetime effort when he wasn't devouring grad students for shoddy work, and peanut size intellects."

"But I'm not really a UW student."

"He knows that. That's what's so intriguing to the good professor. You've peaked his interest being a Wilson High student and all. It turns out Professor Richmond is an alumni of the school, as well as the football team. Played in the line. Big guy. Nice coincidence, don't you think?"

"My curiosity in trains and court cases?"

"Funny mixture. But, yes, he liked that, too."

Garvey and his dad were driving the short distance from their home to the University of Washington's main campus in Seattle. Known as UW to its legions of devoted football fans, the school was the heart and soul of the city, especially when the Trojans of Southern Cal paid a visit. At such times, if the late fall weather cooperated, the color purple, the school's color, competed with brilliant white snowdrifts for the eye's attention. And that's where Gramps' last cue had taken them --- "163 U.S. 537" --- to the home of the Huskies. Garvey's dad had figured the cue out immediately, though he had made his son extract the information number-by-number, letter-by-letter. Pulling teeth without a shot of painkiller would have been easier, or so Garvey came to believe. As to why parents afflict such love on their children that was a question Garvey cared not to look at. What mattered was what he now understood the clue. In law book 163, U.S. Supreme Court cases, beginning on page 537 was the answer, a court case related by some invisible line to the 555th Airborne.

They were comfortably warm in the new Dodge Alaskan four-wheel jeep that Garvey's dad loved to drive. One day soon Garvey hoped to drive it too after he took his driving test. Most probably, he would drive a little faster than his middle-aged, middle class father. Naturally, he would listen to different music. This, it seemed, was a DMV generational thing. That aside, each noticed that it was a beautiful, brisk fall day with clear skies and a moderate 45 degrees with no chance for rain, at least for two days. And that was something for Seattle.

The trees had already turned, dropping millions of multi-colored leaves on sidewalks and streets throughout the northwestern city, even as a sweeping Canadian wind deposited many more leaves on car roofs, front lawns, and pedestrian umbrellas.

Once the snows came, the reds and browns, and all shades between, would mix with the white flakes creating an ugly slush of wet and dry, discomforting to the eye and certainly no joy to walk in or drive through. But for a moment it was just the leaves that held sway throughout the port city, shed by trees and again renewing the mysterious cycle of life common to them.

"Professor Richmond is in your Mason's group, Dad?"

"Many years. He's about three-levels ahead of me last time I checked. Why do you ask?"

"And you play golf together?"

"Where I'm about three holes better."

"So you're good friends?"

"Certainly. Why all the questions?"

"Is that why he's seeing me, because he knows you?"

"Possibly. One of the reasons anyway… But, Garvey, he really wants to meet you."

Like most almost 16-year old teens from Confucius to today Garvey wanted to do things on his own in the spirit of developing independence, and yet still know his parents "had his back" in in case things didn't work out. He needed to see the professor and his dad had helped make that possible. Still, he wished he could have done it on his own dime. The "teen days," Garvey reflected were a sort of halfway house between the freedom to come and go and the dependency stage in which he was a continuing, fully paid up member. Still and all, he thought, I'm going to see the noted historian, who specialized in the post-Reconstruction decades following the Hayes election.

"There's the main gate, Garvey. Just fall in with the crowd. No one will know you're a high school junior. And you're big. Just act like you own the place. But, if anyone asks, just say you're a prodigy."

"Thanks, Dad."

Ten minutes later, Garvey stood outside of Husky Hall, just a little to the side of the throng shuffling into the building. Taking a deep breath and screwing up his courage, he double-stepped his way into the building and headed for the faculty offices. Presently he found the right door and knocked.

"Enter," came a resounding voice.

Garvey did. Standing before a large and very cluttered desk was a tall, dignified gentleman with closely chopped steel, gray hair, a thick mustache, and penetrating black eyes that seem to flash with wit and understanding. Professor Josiah Richmond was a large man, nearly the height of Garvey's father, about five inches above six feet. He was wearing a light-blue turtleneck shirt, cream-colored, highly creased slacks, and glossy, very polished shoes. Though he was fifty something, the Professor looked strong enough to play middle linebacker for the school's football team, which he had done many moons ago. It should also be noted that he was Black.

Seating himself behind his desk after a hearty shaking of hands that left Garvey's fingers somewhat numb, Professor Richmond then gave Garvey that special look parents seem to reserve for their wayward children, or college professors for their nervous students before final grades were posted. That sort of checking you out look which could stop a train in its tracks. Not yet speaking, the Professor Richmond motioned for Garvey to take a seat. For a long moment nothing was said, youth and the professor perhaps sizing up each other. Then...

"Garvey, at last we meet," Professor Richmond said with a charming smile. "And right on time unlike some of the knuckleheads who are late to my classes."

"Professor..."

"Relax. I don't start eating students until 11:00 p.m. You are pretty safe for three hours."

"I have dispensation for a little time then?"

"And witty, too. Smart and witty, good combination, Just like your father said."

"I appreciate you seeing me."

"Wouldn't miss the opportunity. Always like to talk about Homer."

"Homer?"

"After years of research, I feel like I'm on a first-name basis with Mr. Homer Plessy, Garvey."

"Right, I guess."

"I suspect you would like to know him better, too."

"Yes."

"Then we shall begin with a test."

Here it comes, thought Garvey. He's going to quiz the daylights out of me to find out how little I know. Probably won't want to speak to me after he finds how dense I am. God, why did I push my father so hard for this meeting? I must have been out of my miserable mind.

Though Garvey had been raised as a secular humanist a small prayer did bubble up in his mind's eye: "Whoever might be out there, please don't let me mess up today." A religious conversion it was not. On the other hand, it was a spiritual beginning, if one wanted to see it that way.

"Garvey, look around this office. Look for something cool, something related to our topic of discussion, and tell me about it."

Talk about being vague, Garvey's inner voice said. But it had to be something dealing with Plessy. Otherwise, this game makes no sense. But what was the professor after?

"You're looking?"
"Intently."
"And?"
"I think I see it."
"What?"
"You have a large poster on the wall to my right."
"Three posters to be exact."
"But only one that pays homage to Plessy."
"You recognize it?"
"Yes."
"Tell me about it. From your seat… No peeking."

———————————

"The poster honors Homer Plessy. February 12, 2009, to be exact; that's when he was finally honored by the city of New Orleans, as was the civil rights movement in general. Of course, it was about 113-years after Plessy got into trouble with the New Orleans authorities. Presiding on the recent occasion was Keith Plessy and Phoebe Ferguson, two descendants of the major players in the famous court case. The youthful descendants had established a foundation for the 'Education, Preservation, and Outreach' of information related to civil rights. Their goal was to create new ways to teach history, particularly the historic Plessy v. Ferguson Case, 1890 (163 U.S. 537). They wanted to honor the key figures in the figure in the drama with a historical marker, which was placed at the corner of Press and Royal Streets, where the whole story began."

PHOEBE FERGUSON AND KEITH PLESSY

"Excellent memory. Sharp as a tack, but didn't you leave out something, Garvey?"

"What?"

"What story began at those cross streets?"

"That's where Homer Plessy was arrested."

"Because?"

"He tried to ride in a 'white-only' railroad passenger car."

"Fine. Now tell me about the Keith and Phoebe."

Garvey felt the words flow from his mind. Days of personal research were paying off. He was on solid ground. This wasn't as bad as he thought.

"Keith was a distant relative of the defendant, Plessy. Phoebe was a distant relative of the Louisiana justice who heard the case before it went to the U.S. Supreme Court."

"You do know your history. Now for the big question... What else does it say on the historical marker? You know, the small print."

Ouch, thought Garvey. The professor is really pushing. He wanted to run over to the wall, put on a jeweler's eyepiece, or pull out a magnifying glass that would surely make Sherlock Holmes proud, and then peer as intensely as possible at the poster. Naturally, he couldn't do that. He was glued to the seat under Professor Richmond's watchful eyes. He had recently looked at pictures of the marker. He tried to see it again, beginning from afar, and then quietly creeping up on them, finally seeing the words again, big and bold. Now if his nerves didn't fail him...

———————————

June 7, 1892... The defendant, Homer Adolph Plessy, was removed from a railroad car run by the East Louisiana Railroad Company. Plessy was quickly arrested. A private detective, C.C. Cain, made the arrest. Plessy was immediately charged with violating the 1890 Louisiana Separate Car Act, which required passengers to be separated on the basis of race. Plessy's act of civil disobedience was to prove a test case in order to determine the constitutionality of the Louisiana act. Unfortunately, the state court ruled against Plessy, as did the U.S. Supreme Court on appeal, May 18, 1895.

REMEMBERING THE PAST

"Again, well done, Garvey. Your dad was right. You do have a first rate mind, and, it would appear, something of a photographic memory. Excellent. Let's test it a bit more. What is the quote on the marker? How the defense felt about its loss."

"Something about, 'We as freemen still…'"

"We as freemen still believe we are right and our cause is sacred. In defending the cause of liberty; we met with defeat but not with ignominy."

"Well done, Professor Richmond."

"You're now grading me."

"Merely applauding your recall."

"And a politician, too. You'll get along well with the professors in this university, if you choose to attend. For now, a last question, Garvey, before we get to your questions. How long did it take before the Plessy decision would be overturned? How long before Plessy would be vindicated? How many years?"

"About 58-years, not until 1952 and the Brown v. Board of Education case."

"And what doctrine would be ended by this second case?"

"Separate but equal."

This kid was on the ball, Professor Richmond, thought to himself. Really on the ball... He's done his homework. He knows the facts. He's got the dates down. He's acquainted with the names and the court's decisions. But does he understand the implications of what he knows? He's so young. Time will tell, he admonished himself. I'll find out. Just maybe I've found a budding historian. That would be nice, a youngster who really cared about history.

"Okay, Garvey. You've passed my tests. Now what's on your mind?"

"A few questions to fill in my research."

"For a research paper?"

"For my A.P. U.S. History class."

"And for you, Garvey?"

"I need to know why some Black men were willing to leap into the sky?"

"Ah, an interesting way to put it. The 555th?"

"Yes. But how did you know?"

"Golfing partners talk."

"Parents?"

The professor chuckled. "Reserve your adolescent angst. Let's begin. Question #1 I can guess. You want to know more about Homer Plessy?"

"Enough to fill in the blanks. Yes. My sources were vague."

"He was born Homere-Pateric Plessy in New Orleans on March 17, 1862 just prior to Lincoln's Emancipation Proclamation. His parents, long forgotten, were Joseph Adolphe Plessy and Rosa Debergue. They were members of a unique group, 'the free people-of-color caste' of New Orleans."

"Really?"

"History ran in the family. Plessy's paternal grandfather was Germain Plessy, a white Frenchman born in Bordeaux in 1777. Somehow he got to Haiti and then arrived in New Orleans with other Haitian expatriates who fled the island in wake of the slave rebellion led by Toussaint L'Ovuerture. That was the revolt that freed Haiti from Napoleon in the 1790's. Germain Plessy married Catherine Mathieu, who was a free woman of color. They had eight children, including Homer Plessy's father, Joseph Adolphe Plessy.'

"I never knew."

"So what do we have, Garvey? Obviously, Plessy came from a mixed family, French and African His family was part of the free-people-of-color caste of New Orleans. Finally, he was a non-slave. His parents were reasonably well educated for the day. He experienced a middle class life style, as Blacks understood it during the post-Civil War days. This was the world in which Plessy grew up. Eventually, he would enter into a variety of occupations: shoemaker, laborer, clerk, and insurance agent. In passing, another footnote should be referenced. Unfortunately, Plessy's father died when the boy was seven years old. His mother, Rosa Debergue Plessy, a seamstress remarried. Her new husband, Victor M. Dupart, was a clerk for the U.S. Post Office in New Orleans, who supplemented his income by repairing shoes, and imparting these skills to his stepson.

"Homer Plessy married in 1888. He was twenty-five years old. He married Louise Bordenave, a nineteen-year old. They were married in New Orleans. Father Joseph Subileau of St. Augustine Church officiated. His employer served as a witness. The couple took up residence at 1108 North Claiborne Avenue in New Orleans, where the new husband registered to vote in the Sixth Ward's Third Precinct. He was a free man with his wife in the Deep South. What could be better?"

"The details... Professor, how can you remember so much?"

"Three reasons, Garvey. First, I knew you were coming? Second, I had time to refresh my 'little gray cells.' Lastly, as I said before, I'm on a first name basis with Homer. We spent, I dare say, years becoming friends. I sometimes think I know more about him than myself."

"Still."

"What is important, Garvey, is this: do you have some understanding of the man, something more than mere details? What made the man tick? What made him do what he did? After all, he never toiled in the cotton fields or felt the whip of slavery. He never farmed. He always lived in an urban area, and always as a free man. His first language wasn't even English. French was spoken in his home. He always had a skilled occupation or a professional income. And, of course, he was an 'octoroon.'"

"A what?"

"Caught you, have I?"

"In triplicate. What is it? Sounds like an acquaintance of Tarzan, something swinging through a lush African jungle."

"It was a word to describe an archaic method by which to categorize people of mixed-races on the basis of race by using the 'one-drop rule.'"

"Never heard of it."

Sadly, I fear, your education is about to be enriched. If you had one drop of African blood, you were classified as Black. In Plessy's case, since he had a great-grandfather who was African, he was considered 'seven-eighths-white,' but still Black by one drop. By this method, of course, I'm an octoroon, as are you, Garvey, since we each came from a mixed family. It was a crude way of assigning children of mixed unions to an ethnic group, which was perceived by the dominant social group as being subordinate. In other words, it was a measuring stick used by whites to define Blacks."

"And in Louisiana, as one-drop Blacks, we would have been subject to the Jim Crow policies of the state."

"Question, Garvey, or statement?"

"Reality."

"Sadly, throughout the South and into the next century. We would have borne the brunt of "Jumping Jim Crow.""

"You know about him, Professor?"

"Oh, yes. Through my research, we have shadowed each other for years. We are, I suppose you could say, almost like brothers."

CHAPTER 9

FIRST CLASS TICKET

Garvey pondered what he had just heard. For the first time, he really felt some sort of historical tie to Homer Plessy and the Army paratroopers he had researched while in high school. The feeling had been growing in him, first as a tiny itch to know about the 555th, later to just understand the backdrop to why these men wanted to be parachutists during WWII, but now it was something more. History had caught up to him. He was now attached to the 555th by skin color, by race, and by the past. The itch was now a thirst to know the whole story, whatever its ugliness, and, hopefully, whatever transcending good had emerged because of those young men who fought a battle for human dignity long before he was born. He wondered if Gramps knew all this would take place?

"Perhaps I can interrupt your musings, Garvey. What's next on the agenda? Surely, you have more questions."

"Political involvement… How did Plessy get involved in this railroad business? How did he end up before the U.S. Supreme Court? I know something of this, but not enough.

"More than one question, but all tied together."

―――――――――――

"Plessy's road to civil rights activist, and that is what he became, begins with his stepfather, who was a signatory to the 1873 Unification Movement, which took hold during Reconstruction and especially in New Orleans. This political effort sought to establish principles of racial equality in Louisiana. The "movement" was a call to action to end discrimination and segregation. The 100-member organization consisted of Blacks and whites, Jews and Gentiles, all brought together by the need to end biased laws based on skin color. Simply put, they believed "color" should not be a barrier to where you ate, sat, or lived among others. With Hayes' disputed victory in 1876, and the emergence of harsh Jim Crow laws, the movement ended. But in the post-Hayes' period it took new forms, such as the ACERA in New Orleans (American Citizen's Equal Rights Association).

"A Citizens' Committee developed in New Orleans, the most liberal community in the South. At a time when most American Blacks were poor, uneducated, rural laborers, or either ex-slaves or the descendants of slaves, the city was 'home to a large number of relatively affluent, educated professionals,' many of whom were descendant from generations of freemen. The members of these groups were 'eager, determined, and persistent' in their search for racial equality. They were not about to accept Jim Crowism without a fight. The Citizens' Committee was also known by its French name, the Comite'des Citoyens, a civil rights organization made up of Blacks, whites, and Creoles. It was into this group that Homer Plessy migrated.

"At the age of thirty, Plessy was younger than most members of the Comite' des Citoyens. Unlike other members of the organization, he did not have literary prowess, business acumen, or law degrees. He was at that time a shoemaker. Apparently, he wanted to make an impact on society that was more than simply making shoes. Perhaps because of his stepfather, he was already displaying a social awareness concerning the injustices of discriminatory Jim Crow laws. In any event, Plessy, passionate and highly motivated, did have one outstanding attribute that others considered important, especially for the assignment they had in mind for him."

"Well, Garvey, any thought about this? What his special attribute might be? What would make him so important?"

The Plessy files were turning over fast in Garvey's mind. One idea after another was rejected. One point after another was excluded. Soon, almost too soon, only one possibility remained. It made sense, he thought. It was a necessary prerequisite to what happened on the train anyway. It was the key to the arrest.

"Yes."
"Well?"
"Plessy could pass as white. Unless he volunteered the information no one would know he was a Black man"
"Was that enough, pigmentation invisibility?"
"Yes if he was educated and he was. Yes if he conducted himself in a certain manner and he did. Yes if he spoke in a certain way."
"Your final answer?"
"Yes."
"Then I'll get on with the story."

––––––––––––––

"In 1892 Plessy volunteered for a mission that would change his life, creating unpredictable consequences and backlashes within the redeemed Southern states, if not the entire country. It all began on June 7th.

"Plessy, at the urging of others, volunteered to consciously break the law by challenging the Louisiana's Separate Car Law that required the segregation of passengers by race on all railroads within the state. Plessy's task was divided into four parts. First, he was to purchase a first-class ticket on the East Louisiana Railroad running between New Orleans and Covington. With the physical features of a white male, he would have no trouble doing this. The fact that Plessy could infiltrate the whites-only car without encountering any resistance would highlight the arbitrary, if not subjective nature of the state's law.

"Second, he was to board the train and, as required and expected, take a seat in the 'whites-only' passenger car. Again, he passed this test without a hitch. He drew no attention. His fellow passengers had no idea that he, a white-looking gentleman, was taking part in one of the most famous acts of civil disobedience in American history, Rosa Parks notwithstanding.

"Third, he was to get arrested. Everything depended on this. He would do this by informing the conductor who came to collect his ticket that he, Homer Plessy, was 7/8 white. Conveniently and of his own volition, Plessy was saying, "I'm a Black man." When, as it was assumed, the conductor asked him to leave the "white only car," he would refuse. This was absolutely necessary. This was to be explained to the conductor without rancor in a dignified manner. Plessy was to keep his cool regardless of the conductor's response, or that of the other white passengers. The conductor, it was hoped, would call for police assistance if a law enforcement person happened to be on the train. As it turns out there was a detective present. His name was Chris C. Cain. From the conductor's point-of-view, this was a very fortuitous situation. He was immediately asked to arrest Plessy. This was quickly done to the satisfaction of whites riding on the train, and, of course, to Plessy.

"Only the fourth task remained. Plessy needed to be booked. He was not to resist charges or booking. Indeed, it was essential for this to occur. This was also done. He was escorted off the train and put into the Orleans Parish jail. He faced a fine of $25.00 or up to 20 days in jail, the penalties for sitting in the wrong passenger car. However, Plessy would only spend one night in jail before being released the next day on a $500 bond put up by the Comite' des Citovens."

"Wow."

"Wow, Garvey… That's all you have to say?"

"My all-purpose word for 'that's fantastic.'"

"If you say so. Perhaps you're ready for a real WOW!"

"Try me."

"The entire four-part episode and looming court trials was done with the complete cooperation and prior knowledge of East Louisiana Railroad."

"What?"

"I'll take that as WOW-WOW!"

"The railroad was in league with the Citizens' Committee?"

"Up to its smoke stacks."

"How could that be?"

"The railroad was caught between that famous hard spot and a rock. On the one hand, it needed to make a profit. It had investors. On the other hand, the company had to abide by Jim Crow laws. The Separate Car Act challenged profits. Scarce funds were needed to purchase additional cars in order to separate the races on every train. Extra workers were needed to enforce the law, especially when only one passenger car was available. If both races were seated in the same car, a partition, usually a curtain was drawn between Blacks and whites in order to separate them. More conductors were needed for this. If two cars were available, two conductors were still needed. One car for both races was, of course, the answer. For the railroad management, this was the dollar price of compliance with the legislative edict to provide "separate accommodations for white and black passengers. But white supremacy laws were one thing. The profit line was quite another.

"In cooperation with the Citizens' Committee, the special detective, Chris C. Cains was hired by the railroad to ride along with Plessy in order to make sure he was arrested. It was, as we might say, a set-up, prearranged. Even the conductor, many speculate, was in on the orchestrated arrest. That, I must add, has never been proven. The whole episode, however, was choreographed. It was a sophisticated charade. No adventure novelist could have done better.

"Both the Committee and the railroad hoped that a state court case would 'vindicate Plessy by overturning the railroad segregation law as unconstitutional.' Were this to happen, the entire edifice of Jim Crowism in the South might collapse. So much hinged, then, on what the state courts would do as the light of the U.S. Constitution shone on the Louisiana law. A great deal was at stake."

A STRANGE TRAIN

"I think I'll need a new adjective, Professor Richmond. Wow doesn't seem to catch the spirit of what really happened."

"Tell me, Garvey, what are you feeling?"

"Feeling?"

"A simple question. Your emotions, beyond the facts?"

"I'm angry."

"At?"

"The past."

"Understandable, since you're from a mixed family, too."

"Because about 150-years ago, I couldn't ride first class on the East Louisiana Railroad. And because my color, if I were not sufficiently light, I would be marked as a Black, a "one-drop" person of color. Because 'Jumping Jim Crow' was jumping all over me."

"That was long ago."

"I'm still Black."

"As am I, Garvey. We're one-drop buddies, so to speak. But we've come along way. Not easily, not without pain, but progress has been made, not fully, not completely, but significantly better than in Plessy's time."

"What are you really saying, Professor Richmond?"

"Find some balance, Garvey. Go a little Buddhist. Accept some perspective. Resist the temptation to see the world in straight lines, black and white. And control the anger. What happened, well it happened. It can't be undone. But we can understand it. We can learn from it. We can avoid letting it happen again."

"Not easy to do."

"True enough. But a good historian doesn't write dispassionately. He's entitled to his feelings. And certainly subjectivity enters the picture. But, Garvey, he commands himself to write with as much objectivity as possible, to go where the facts take him, to look at all sides, and to reach conclusions devoid of personal feelings to the extent possible. And most of all, a good historian tries valiantly to not judge the past too harshly on the basis of contemporary values and customs. And he never lets the toxic notion of 'political correctness' enter his thought processes."

"No anger?"

"Control it. No wild horses. No thundering across the landscape of history trying to seek vengeance with the pen, or should I say the computer, trying to settle old scores between the covers of a history book, hoping to redress what cannot be undone."

"Why are you telling me all this?"

"Because you're young. Because, Garvey, you have the potential to be a fine history student, if you decided to major along that line, and because you have the makings of a historian. And perhaps because, young man, I'm getting older. I would like to hope you're in the pipeline. And because, as Black-Americans, we need to have Black historians, not an unblemished past, but rather to set the record straight, candidly, fairly, intellectually."

"And you think I can?"

"Oh, yes. The potential is there. Now, enough of all that... Let's see what you know about the court cases. Your turn, Garvey."

Here Garvey felt he was on strong ground. He had been fascinated by the Plessy court case, devouring all he could find to appease his interest. He was conversant with the key issues.

———————————

"Plessy's case went before Judge John Howard Ferguson about one month after his arrest. The attorney for the Committee, Albion Winegar Tourgee, an experienced civil rights lawyer for his day, represented Plessy. He was perhaps 'the most outspoken white radical on the race question in the late 1880's.' He had called for resistance to the Louisiana law in his well-read newspaper column, *A Bystander's Notes,* which was syndicated in many newspapers across the country. It was in this way that he became known to the 'Black press' for his bold denunciations of lynching, segregation, disfranchisement, white supremacy, and scientific racism. It's no wonder he was the Committee's first choice to represent Plessy

"Well stated. Go on."

"Tourgee argued that Plessy's civil rights, as granted by the Thirteenth and Fourteenth amendments of the U.S. Constitution, had been violated. Judge Ferguson rejected the argument. He ruled that under state law, Louisiana had the 'power to set rules that regulated railroad business within its borders.' The Louisiana State Supreme Court affirmed Judge Ferguson's ruling and refused to grant a rehearing. It did allow, however, a petition for a writ of error. Technically, this is a document issued by an appellate court (a court of appeals) to the court of record where a case was tried, 'requiring that the record of the trial be sent to the appellate court for examination of alleged errors.' In time, the U.S. Supreme Court accepted this petition. Four years later, in April 1896, the case of Plessy v. Ferguson began."

"Excellent. Continue."

"Again, Tourgee argued that the state of Louisiana had violated the Thirteenth Amendment, which granted 'freedom to the slaves,' and the Fourteenth Amendment, which stated, 'no state shall make or enforce any law which shall abridge the privileges or immunities of citizens of the United States, nor shall any state deprive any person of life, liberty, and property, without due process of law.'"

"A persuasive argument, young man. Did the Supreme Court buy Tourgee's plea?"

"The ruling of the Supreme Court was handed down by a vote of 7 to 1 with the majority opinion written by Justice Henry Billings Brown. The lone dissenter was Justice John Marshall Harlan, who wrote the minority opinion. Specially, the Court upheld the constitutionality of state laws requiring racial segregation in public facilities under the doctrine of 'separate but equal.' Though the narrow verdict applied to private railroads wholly within a state, the doctrine, by extension, was expanded to include public facilities throughout the redeemed states of the former Confederacy. This ruling became the standard doctrine in U.S. law until its repudiation in the 1954 Supreme Court decision in Brown v. Board of Education. Upon hearing the decision, the Committee of Citizens replied, as you know: 'We, as freemen, still believe that we are right and our cause is sacred.'"

"Well done, Garvey."

"Thanks. But at this point I need some help, Professor."

"We all do from time to time. Permit me to assist. The Court stated the Fourteenth Amendment 'offered no protection of social rights.' Continuing, the majority opinion maintained that, 'if one race be inferior to the other socially, the Constitution of the United States cannot put them on the same plane.' Rather explicitly, the Court rejected the notion put forth by Plessy that 'segregation was inherently demeaning.' The ruling challenged the so-called victims of racial prejudice, describing as a fallacy the idea that 'the enforced separation of the two races stamps the colored race with a badge of inferiority.' Going on, the Court said, 'If this be so, it is not by reason of anything found in the act, but solely because the colored race chooses to put that construction upon it.'"

"Ouch."

"Why ouch?"

"Because of the paradox."

"Oh?"

"Didn't separating the races in public schools follow?"

"Indeed, Garvey."

"But the schools were not equal. Wasn't that the case?"

"That's true."

"So the Black kids could never catch up to the white students."

"So that's the paradox?"

"I think so. It's like applying for a job. The employer wants people with experience. But you need a job to get experience."

"Meaning?"

"Separate but equal was basically unequal when it came to public education. "

"Catch your breath, Garvey. I'm not going anywhere."

"That was sort of like blaming the victim for being a victim."

"You might say that. But, again, calm yourself."

"Once I started, the information just flowed out of me like a river after a torrential rain."

"An historical flood, if I may use your metaphor."

"And I hope accurate."

"So far, yes. Please continue, Garvey."

"The minority report of the Supreme Court, as already noted, was given by Justice Harlan. Ironically, he was a southerner and former slaveholder compared to Judge Brown, who was from Massachusetts and had never owned slaves. What a paradox! Brown, the judge from a definitely Union state, defended 'separate but equal," while a southerner, Marshall opposed the concept."

JOHN MARSHALL HARLAN

"That's the joy of history. You never know what's going to pop out once you stir the tea leaves of the past."

"In his dissent, Marshall said, "segregation was a 'badge of servitude' and inherently degrading to Black citizens. He wrote:

In the eye of the law, there is in this country no superior, dominant, ruling class of citizens. There is no caste here. Our constitution is color-blind, and neither knows nor tolerates classes among citizens.' Continuing, he said, 'in respect to civil rights, all citizens are equal before the law.'

"He added:

The humblest is the peer of the most powerful. The law regards man as man, and takes no account of his surroundings or of his color when his civil rights as guaranteed by the supreme law of the land are involved...

Concluding, Justice Harlan said:

We boost of the freedom enjoyed by our people above all other peoples. But is difficult to reconcile the boast with a state of the law, which, practically, puts the brand of servitude and degradation upon a large class of our fellow citizens, our equals before the law. The thin disguise of 'equal' accommodations for passengers in railroad coaches will not mislead any one, nor atone for the wrong this day done.

"Harlan's ringing defense of civil rights was at least half a century too soon. In 1896, the overwhelming majority of the America people did tolerate classes among citizens based on many things, including race. The Supreme Court was not immune from this view. Given that, the Court's ruling essentially protected Jim Crow laws from further constitutional challenges for many decades."

"Again, well done, Garvey. Your review was quite good. Perhaps a question or two on my part."

"Fire away."

"What about the Thirteenth Amendment? Didn't it apply to this case?"

"According to the majority of judges, no. Their view was that the Louisiana statute did not conflict with the amendment, which abolished slavery and involuntary servitude, 'except as a punishment for crime.' The Plessy case was not about slavery or servitude or any state of bondage. The amendment had nothing to do with any rights that were curtailed in the pursuit of 'life, liberty and property.' In such cases where freedom was dramatically restricted, the Fourteenth Amendment would come into play."

"Talk to me about that amendment."

"There are at least three purposes of the Fourteenth Amendment. The first was to establish citizenship of former slaves. This was not an issue in the Plessy case. The second purpose was to provide a definition of citizenship. Again, this was not a question before the Court. Plessy was a citizen. He had been born in the United States. No one challenged that. The third purpose was to protect the 'privileges and immunities of citizens' from hostile state legislation. This third point was the issue before the Court."

"And?"

"Here I'll need your assistance, Sir."

"Of course. The Court pointed out that the Fourteenth Amendment sought only to enforce equality of the two races before the law. It was not intended to abolish distinctions based upon color, or to 'enforce social equality, or the co-mingling of the two races upon terms unsatisfactory to either.' In other words, citizens were entitled to 'due process of law,' and to the 'equal protection of the laws,' but little more. The logic here was that laws permitting, or even requiring the separation of the races were constitutional and did not 'necessarily imply the inferiority of either race.' Such laws were within the 'scope of the states' police powers."

"Understand?"

"Yes, I think so."

"Now a tough question; your feelings about 'separate but equal?'"

Garvey considered the question. Back to feelings… The professor was pushing hard. It must be important to him. Naturally, he could only respond on the basis of youth and an upbringing devoid of the racial restrictions Plessy dealt with in his time. Still, what were his feelings? What was he really feeling?

"Unfairly from my point-of-view, Professor, the Court refused Plessy's challenge by their interpretation of the law and our constitutional rights. The seven justices forming the majority opinion shattered any hope of a judicial response to Jim Crowism sufficient to strike down segregation-inspired legislation. That is, where laws provided for the separation of the races there would be no protection from the 'equal protection clause'_of the Fourteenth Amendment. According to the Court, 'separate but equal' was not only constitutional, but the most reasonable approach considering the social attitudes of the time."

"Reasonable approach, Garvey?"

"What whites could handle at the time and what custom and traditions were permitted in daily life. What the social mores allowed."

"Even if discriminatory?"

"Plessy was taking on 25-years of post Civil War history. He was challenging prejudices and biases. Not an easy thing to do."

"You're justifying 'separate but equal?'"

"No. Just trying to understand what Plessy was dealing with. Like you told me, I'm trying to maintain my balance and objectivity."

"Controlling your anger?"

"Trying."

"Clamping down on your outrage?'

"Again, trying."

"Pushing aside your sense of injustice?"

"Yes, but not easily."

"Good. Once more, Garvey, well stated... Perhaps you would consider a double major at UW?"

"Double major?"

"History major and law student. You were born to do one or the other, if not both. Before you answer, consider this. I want you in my graduate seminar class next semester. It's about this case."

"I better pass my A.P. History class first. College majors will come later."

"Wise thinking. Consider doing both. I keep one seat open for you. Now a few last questions. When you boil it down, what was Justice Henry Brown's view of the races, certainly of the Constitution? And how did it differ from Harlan's view of the races? That ties into this whole question of constitutional rights."

Garvey realized he was being tested again. Pass or fail might hinge on his answers.

"Justice Brown stated that the law does not 'discriminate among legal rights by race, but merely recognizes a distinction between races, which must always exist so long as white men are distinguished from the other race by color.' Additionally, 'legislation is powerless to eradicate racial instincts or to abolish distinctions based on physical differences.'"

"And?"

"If the civil and political rights of both races are equal, one cannot be inferior to the other civilly or politically. If one race is inferior to the other socially the Constitution of the United States cannot put them on the same plane.' This was a subtle way of accepting the notion of 'separate but equal' in schools, railcars, and even drinking fountains --- everywhere the grasp of Jim Crow laws could reach."

"Meaning?"

"Justice Harlan did not advocate social equality among the races. Instead, he argued that, 'legally imposed segregation denied political equality.' Nailing the issue on the head, he wrote:

Everyone knows that the statute in question had its origin in the purpose, not so much to exclude white persons from railroad cars occupied by blacks, as to exclude colored people from coaches occupied by or assigned to white persons.

Garvey paused for a moment. He knew he was on the right track. Using a football metaphor he hoped he could cross the goal line.

"Harlan refuted the view that the Louisiana law discriminately equally among Blacks and whites. For Harlan, then, "separate but equal" was unattainable, since there could be no equality in separation with regard to constitutional rights. In continuing his eloquent dissent, Harlan looked to the future, implying that 'separate but equal' was a system 'inconsistent with the guarantee given by the Constitution to each State of a republican form of government, and may be stricken down by congressional action, or by the courts in the discharge of their solemn duty to maintain the supreme law of the land.' Essentially, he predicted a future Court would undo the Plessy decision."

"Was Justice Harlan right, Garvey?"

"Of course. The Warren Court came along in 1954. As predicted, this court undid the Plessy decision. It's a matter of record."

"Excellent recitation. You're continuing to put my doctoral candidates to shame, Garvey. Your dad said you were smart as a whip. Was he ever right."

"My dad said that?"

"And not in a moment of weakness."

"Really?"

"Gospel truth."

"Wow."

"We're back to that, are we?"

"Perhaps I should say, 'Holy Cow,' but I have no idea what that means."

"Nor do I. But I have one last question."

"A last question, Professor Richmond?"

"What was written on the other side of the plaque honoring Homer Plessy? Unfortunately, I don't have a large poster, but I do have a small picture. Well, Garvey?"

"I've never seen the back of the plaque."

"Honestly stated. Care to take a guess, Garvey."

"The back side explained, I would think, when he was born and when he died, perhaps even where he's buried. "

"Is that all?"

"It might say something about one of the Court justices."

"Which one?"

"Harlan comes to mind because of his dissent, but…"

"But?"

"I'll vote for Justice Ferguson."

"Why?"

"It was Plessy v. Ferguson."

The dinner dishes were washed and put away, a necessary ritual in a busy household. Garvey's twin siblings, Wells and Harlan were upstairs in their rooms doing their homework. At least that was the hope. Three years younger than Garvey, the "twins" could be a handful with their strong personalities, active minds, and the seemingly unlimited ways they could get at their older brother. Tonight, however, Garvey wanted none of that. He was rehashing his day with Professor Richmond. His parents were unusually attentive.

"So that's it."
"Wow."
"My exact word, dad."
"He wants you to be a lawyer?"
"And a professor of history, mom."
"At UW?"
"Huskie-land for me, dad."
"And he wants you to take his seminar class next fall? With all those graduate students?"
"Dad, that's what he said."
"And will you?"
"Of course, mom. Just think of it. One whole semester studying American history, 1965 – 1900, the reconstruction period on steroids."

It was obvious to Garvey that his parents were proud of him. He rejoiced in this delightful form of affection. He also realized he had earned their praise. He had worked hard. Research takes time. Though his classes hadn't suffered, his social life had, particular with one particular cheerleader. Trade offs… Always trade offs. His mother broke into his thoughts.

"Garvey, we have three questions."
"Shoot."
"What happened to Homer Plessy?
"Yes?"
"What's the story behind Keith Plessy and Phoebe Ferguson?"
"And the last question?"
"And what's the next cue from you know who?"

––––––––––––––––––––

"As to Homer Plessy's later life… It appears he disappeared in relative anonymity befitting a father and husband, who had to support his family. We know he went to work for the People's Life Insurance Company, a Black owned company, for which he sold insurance premiums. Apparently, he also continued to be involved in religious and social issues important to the Black community. He died in 1925 on March 1st. He was buried in the family tomb in New Orleans' St. Louis Cemetery.

"It should be noted that after the Supreme Court decided his case Plessy reported to the Ferguson court to answer the charge of violating the Separate Car Act. He changed his plea from innocent to guilty and paid the $25 fine.

"Keith Plessy was the decedent of the man who tested the Louisiana law requiring separate railroad cars for whites and Blacks. He first learned about his famous last name when he was in elementary school. He was a native of New Orleans. He was a graduate of John McDonogh High School and the New Orleans Center for Creative Arts. Acclaimed as a gifted artist he had painted a hundred portraits of leaders in the civil rights movement. The paintings were done on the interior walls of schools and can be seen today. Most of his energy and effort today is with the Plessy-Ferguson Foundation where he works diligently with civil rights activists and educators.

"Pheobe Ferguson was the great-great-great granddaughter of the judge (John Howard Ferguson) who upheld the Louisiana law. She was also a native of New Orleans. For over 20-years she was a highly successful photographer and filmmaker in New York City. She returned to New Orleans partially because of Hurricane Katrina. She drove a truck full of supplies from Brooklyn, New York to the stricken city, where she made a documentary about the disaster. She has remained in New Orleans making contemporary films.

"Plessy and Ferguson came together to put the past behind them by creating the Plessy and Ferguson Foundation in New Orleans to improve race relations. Together they agreed that the past cannot be undone, but it can be acknowledged and understood. This is what they wish to do through their Foundation."

"And the next clue, Garvey?"

"I'm going to disappoint you, Mom. Gramps didn't give me one. In fact, he shared his research with me, really just rough notes needing a lot of work, but with a great story. A few more days and I'll have everything pieced together. I never knew about the things he included in his files. Made me proud of the guys."

"What guys, Garvey?"

"Dad, the guys who leaped into the sky."

CHAPTER 10

THE DELEGATION

Garvey had worked his way through Gramps' notes. It had not been easy. If he had a system, it was not apparent. Garvey quickly realized he needed to approach the mass of material as if he was completing a puzzle. First, find the edges, then look for like-minded colors or patterns, and slowly piece together a picture that made sense. It took some effort but in time it paid off. A picture did emerge.

It was time to share with his parents and his new mentor.

Garvey was excited, almost coming out of his Nike shoes. He glanced around the kitchen table. A pile of neatly, double spaced typing was before him, as were his parents and Professor Richmond. As usual, Wells and Harlan were elsewhere, this time assisting the local Salvation Army serve dinner to those in need. Part of their school's effort to include community service in the curriculum. As for Garvey and others at the table, a fried chicken dinner was over and the hot apple pie dessert was dispensed with obvious relish. Now all eyes were on him.

Researching the 555th was now more than an assignment for Garvey. Prompted by Gramps and Professor Richmond Garvey had crossed some invisible line, what people might refer to a Rubicon. Whatever it was he was determined to know all he could about these Black men who leaped into the empty skies. Who were they? How did their unit come about? What was the story behind the history? Had he had access to a time machine, compliments of H.G. Wells, Garvey would have certainly used it. And what he would have learned first hand. Still, he had learned much from Gramps's research trove.

"We're ready, Garvey."

"Hopefully, I am, too, Dad."

"Lets have it, my budding history scholar," Professor Richmond said with a gleam in his eyes.

"Okay. Time to delve deeply into the past and the origins of the 555th. To do that we need to go back a few years, and I need to tell a story."

JANUARY 1940 - THE WHITE HOUSE

The old Plymouth taxicab, all V-8 cylinders still purring smoothly, quietly stopped in front of the White House. It did so, of course, because two very large, tough-looking Marines with apparently loaded rifles, tipped with bayonets, told the cabbie to halt. Surprisingly, the Marines were very spry considering it was 5:00 a.m. in a chilly morning. Apparently, when you guard President Franklin D. Roosevelt, you stay on your toes, even through a long night, punctuated by a light rain and temperatures dipping into the low 40's. Of course, the taxi would have stopped even without a Marine detachment. Cement barriers blocked any further vehicular movement, at least on this side entrance to the so-called "people's house." No doubt the heavy security made sense given Roosevelt's lack of popularity in some quarters of the country, and the small fact that the nation was half-a-step from being dragged into another European war.

One of the Marines, loosely cloaked in a khaki poncho, yelled, "Out" in a husky voice brooking no dissent. And out they came, three elderly Negroes, each clutching a small envelope in one hand and an unopened umbrella in the other.

"Harry, more cooks for the White House."
"Could be more custodians, Zack."
"Might be gardeners."
"Whatever. They sure are dressed spiffy."

Indeed they were. Each wore a three-piece dark suit with light-colored lines accentuating the jacket and pants. Dark shoes, nicely polished, ensconced their feet, while a dark fedora hat covered their salted mix of black and white hair marking them as older men. In unison they handed their envelopes to the Marine called Zack.

"What's this," he asked crustily?"
"Our ticket to enter," one of the men said a little impatiently. Perhaps you'd like to look at it."
"Watch your tone, boy."
"As you can plainly see, I'm old enough to be your father, which makes the term 'boy' rather inappropriate,' the tallest of the group said.
"Smart Black ass."
"You're keeping the President waiting."
"You're kidding," exclaimed Harry. "The President interviewing the hired help now?"
"Again, I ask you to check the note inside."
"Check it, Zack."
Zack grabbed one envelop, pried it open, quickly read the note inside, and then repeated the process two more times before exclaiming, "Well, I'll be damned."
"What'd got?"
"Invites."

A moment later another Marine joined them, checked the notes, and then escorted the three men into a side entrance of the White House.

Outside, still cold, tired, and wet, Zack said, "Can you beat that, three old Negroes heading for the Oval Office?"

"Niggers, you mean. That's what we say in Mississippi."

"Well, don't say it too loudly here. Mrs. Roosevelt doesn't like that word."

The three Negroes never got to the Oval Office, nor did they expect to. They knew they were meeting with representative of the President in a side office, which some might consider out-of-the-way. Certainly, meeting at this hour suggested an attempt to keep the meeting private. In short, no newspaper boys and no public announcements. Blacks visitors in the White House, that wasn't something advertised in a country where race, elections, and votes intersected at 1600 Pennsylvania Avenue in 1940. The three men hoped to meet with Francis Perkins, the Secretary of Labor, but she was unavailable. Also unable to meet with them was the Secretary of War, Henry L. Stimson. This, too, seemed to be an effort to keep the meeting out of the limelight. Emissaries of each, however, were available. It was enough, if what the men had to say was communicated to the secretaries and the President.

As understood the emissaries met with the three men. Pleasantries were exchanged, coffee and coffee cake were provided, and, once the White House help departed and doors to the office were shut, the business of the meeting began.

The three men explained to the political aides why they were there. The tallest of the three said, "We're here to share with the President our concerns about the Negro vote in the upcoming Presidential election."

"Share or pressure," Stimson's surrogate asked?

"Advise."

"Well?"

"We want the President to take action."

"Such as?"

"Desegregate the armed forces."

"Something easy, I see," Perkin's aide replied, a slight smile on his face.

"This is needed to bring about social change and to improve race relations in the country."

"Before you throw up your hands," the shortest of the three Negroes said, "hear us out. Segregation is morally wrong. It embodies an undemocratic doctrine of racial inferiority causing our sons to be denied full opportunities in the military. Because of racial prejudice, Black soldiers are given inferior status and menial jobs, such as cooking, doing common shovel labor, driving trucks, cleaning up the Officers Club, toilets and all."

"But never duty with a gun," the paunchy third man said. "Never an opportunity to go into combat. Too darn much of that in France in 1918, if you will recall? If there's another war, we need to reverse what happened under Pershing. Remember the General, rather than integrate Black soldiers from Harlem, actually attached them to the French Army. And, as I trust you know, they performed valiantly on the Western Front. If my memory doesn't fail me, these soldiers spent more days in continuous combat than any other American unit. Beyond that, they were the first American troops to cross the Rhine and enter Germany. For their extraordinary service, they received the highest honors of the French government."

"The President and the War Department know all that. It's a matter of record."

"As does the Labor Department."

"But nothing is done," the tall man quickly responded. "Just talk, nothing more, while the spirit of our boys declines. You're not letting them be real soldiers. And we don't understand that. Lincoln knew the value of the Black soldier, as did Teddy Roosevelt in the Spanish-American War, and, when given a chance, at times during the First World War. And along the way, as I'm sure you're aware, the Buffalo Soldiers did their job."

"No disagreement there," the War Department representative said. "None at all. But social prejudice may be too great to overcome at this time. Consider that most of our military bases are in the South. Most of our officers were raised in the South. And most of our enlistees are from the South. And pretty much, these folks support a segregated military. What you are asking would be damn difficult to achieve."

"Exactly what is it you want the President to do beyond desegregating the armed force," Labor asked "in order to get the Black vote in November?"

"Crass way to say it," the tall man said.

"But true."

"The President is running for a third term. He's breaking tradition first established by George Washington. His political enemies are many and determined to take him down."

"The Oval Office is aware of this."

"The President will need every Black vote."

"And the price for the Black vote?"

"Promote Colonel Benjamin O. Davis to Brigadier General," the paunchy one stated with zestful satisfaction. "The Black community needs at least one Black general. And it needs more Black officers. And it needs more Black enlistees. Promoting Davis would send the right message to our community."

BENJAMIN O. DAVIS

"Anything else?" Labor responded.

"Appoint William H. Hastie to be an Assistant Secretary in the War Department. The Black community needs a Black man on the inside advocating for our concerns.

WILLIAM H. HASTIE

"You want a lot," the War Department man said. "An awful lot."

"And the President wants the Black vote and this is going to be a tough election, "the short man said. "He's breaking a tradition Washington started, as already pointed out. No one has ever done that before. The opposition is already calling him a tyrant, a Socialist, a dictator, a Commie, a Jew-lover, and worst of all, a traitor to the wealthy class, if not white folks everywhere. And that's just for starters. He's in trouble with the mothers. Pushing conscription, building up the Navy, and putting out war contracts. All signs he's taking the country to war… And facing possibly this guy Wendell Willkie from Indiana. He's already got Lindbergh on his case. You know, his group, American First. Keep America out of another Europe's war."

"Well, he does have the reliable Solid South, Stimson's aide chirped in quickly."

"Because the federal government leaves Jim Crow alone in those states. Southern Democrats support Roosevelt for more than his good looks."

"Democrats the President can't afford to lose in November."

"He can't jeopardize that vote," Perkins aide said. "It's crucial."

"As is winning the Black vote in the north?" the tall Negro asked.

For a moment the air was clear of challenging voices. What had been said defined the political problems of the White House, both to win an election and, at the same time, provide opportunities for Blacks in the military. Differences existed, not about goals, only the tactics.

"Davis and Hastie, maybe," Labor spoke up. "Desegregation of the services, that's another question. The President is sympathetic. And you know where Mrs. Roosevelt stands. But we'd never get it through Congress. Too many folks from the South controlling the committees."

"From the land of Dixie, you mean?"

"And they control votes," Labor added. The President can't get anything out of Congress without their help. You know that. And right now he's trying to get the country prepared for a war he thinks is unavoidable. That takes money. That takes a friendly Congress."

"Exactly, the War Department aide said, raising his voice a bit. The President believes the Phony War in Europe is about to end. The Nazi hordes will attack France. After that, if they can't invade England, they'll try to starve her out. Unrestricted U-boat warfare again. And in the Pacific, the Japs are running all over Manchuria and a good deal of China. Chiang Kai-Shek was barely hanging on. War loomed in the Pacific. The President was trying to think ahead. We may be in a two-ocean war before the year is out. That's his view. That's what the War Department is telling him. He needs the country to rearm. He needs the votes of Southerners in Congress. He has to pick his fights. Who do you want him to fight first, Jim Crow or Hitler?"

"Both," said the tall Negro.

"In the Oval Office, it's not that easy."

"We'll bring your concerns to the President," the man from the War Department said. "Let's see what can be done."

"And tell him this. The Negro will fight and spill blood if necessary to protect our country. Give him the opportunity to do that in combat. Provide him with the chance to fight with dignity and purpose."

History recorded that Benjamin O. Davis got a promotion and, within the limits of his position, advocated for the Black solider. As important as this was, the real coup was Judge William H. Hastie. His appointment to the War Department was of consequence.

Who was Judge William H. Hastie? Why was the Black delegation so determined win his appointment? The simple answer was this. It was hoped he could, if selected for the War Department, revitalize the status and treatment of Blacks in the military. For the delegation he was the right man. On November 1, 1940, a week before Roosevelt won a tough race against his Republican challenger, Hastie was appointed as a Civilian Aid to Secretary of War, Henry L. Stimson. In response to this, Secretary Stimson sent a letter to Hastie charging him with "assisting the War Department in developing administrative policies that would insure the fair and most effective use of Negro manpower in the armed service."

Hastie took up the charge. It was as if his whole life had led to this moment. And indeed, some were convinced, it had. He was born in Knoxville, Tennessee in 1904. He came from a mixed family background. His maternal ancestors were African and Native American. Family tradition held that they were related to a Malagasy princess in Africa. Obviously, very bright, he took to higher education, graduating magna cum laude from Amherst College in Massachusetts. He received his law degree from Harvard Law School in 1930. After practicing law in Washington D.C., he was picked by President Roosevelt to be the first African-American federal judge. Southerners, as expected, opposed FDR on this. Two years later he became the Dean of the Howard University School of Law, as well as being on the faculty. One of his students was future Supreme Court Justice, Thurgood Marshall. He turned out to be the lead attorney in overthrowing the Plessy-Ferguson case years later.

Hastie moved quickly on Stimson's desire to deal with race questions in the armed forces. Hastie recommended "integrating the Army with small cohesive units." No massive effort to desegregate the Army. Rather, Hastie wanted to move slowly, incrementally, and in a controlled manner. He was a realist. Desegregating the military would not be easy. He favored a conservative approach.

Unfortunately, before the War Department could act on the question, the Japanese bombed Pearl Harbor. The United States was at war. Hastie's recommendations were pushed aside. The Army General Staff rejected any form of desegregation. The rationale was that Hastie's proposal was based on "social principles rather than military expertise." The Chief of Staff, George C. Marshall, they said, would not attempt to solve a "major social problem." The Army could not be used as a "social laboratory for effecting social change. The country was at war."

Though disappointed Hastie continued in his efforts to reform the War Department. He requested an increase in the number of Black officers and soldiers in uniform. He requested that Negro soldiers be utilized in areas other than labor and supply units. He recommended that the Army "amplify advertising for the recruitment of Blacks."

Partially influenced by Hastie's efforts, John J. McCloy, the Assistant Secretary of War, formed in August 1942 an Advisory Committee on Negro Troop Policies. Four months later, the committee made two recommendations: "The assignment of Negro Americans to combat arms previously restricted to White Americans." And, the "formation of an all-Negro parachute battalion." Responding to this, Marshall wrote in the margin of the report three words --- "start a company." This was February 1943. In doing so, Marshall was authorizing what would eventually become the 555th Parachute Infantry Battalion.

To some degree, Marshall was responding to what happened one month earlier. Hastie, tired of War Department resistance, resigned his position to protest three problems in particular. First, the continued existence of segregated training facilities in the Army. Second, the continued inadequate training of Black pilots… Third, the unequal distribution of combat assignments between whites and non-whites, even as the fighting worsened and deaths rose. Though unable to resolve these problems during his tenure, he had left his mark on the War Department. The 555ᵗʰ would be his legacy.

Riding home in another Plymouth taxi, the three older Negroes sat quietly in the cab, each absorbed in his own thoughts. As they drove past the Lincoln Memorial, the tallest of them said, "I wonder if we accomplished anything today?"

"Time will tell," the shortest man said."

"Do you think 'old Abe' felt that way, too?" the paunchy man said philosophically, the strain of the meeting still in his voice. "I wonder."

As the taxi sped away from the White House, unstated questions occupied the three men. Assuming that the Army liberalized its policies, where would the Negro recruits come from and would there be enough of them? Would they be able to handle their increased visibility in the white man's Army, and the possibly more challenging training, assuming they had new opportunities? Their questions remained unanswered for the moment.

"Excellent presentation, Garvey," Professor Richmond said, flashing a radiant smile as he did. "Just outstanding research."

"All this came from Gramps' notes?" Garvey's mother asked. "Hard to believe the old guy accumulated all this information."

"This and more, Mom."

"And your independent research, son, let's not forget that."

"Hours in the library, Dad."

"Applause aside, Garvey, you left us with a question. Where would the Negro soldiers come from?"

"Out west, Sir… In the desert wasteland of America."

1943 – FORT HUACHUCA

"His name won't be found in American history textbooks. Just another Army officer in the fall of 1943 given an assignment by those above him… The task might have gone to any of a hundred officers. But it fell to Major Holman D. Hoover, the Adjutant of the Parachute School at Fort Benning, Georgia. He was given the responsibility "for screening and recruiting volunteers, both officers and non-commissioned officers." But not just any men; he would be looking for Negro volunteers. Where to look, of course, was the key question? Fort Benning wouldn't do. None was on the base. The potential volunteers were not there. He would have to look elsewhere. He chose an obscure military base almost completely unknown to the public, Fort Huachuca."

"Obscure is right! Never heard of the place."

"Dad, the fort was located near the town of Sierra Vista in Cochise County, in southeast Arizona. It was about 15-miles north of the border with Mexico. With the spectra of war looming on the horizon, the fort was already preparing for an anticipated buildup of draftees. The fort had an interesting history. On March 3, 1877, Captain Samuel Maraduke Whitside, along with two companies of the 6th Cavalry, chose a site at the base of the Huachuca Mountains that offered "sheltering hills and a perennial stream," a perfect location for a fort. The military was moving into Arizona on a permanent basis."

"Hot and remote… That's the Army for you."

"Professor Richmond, you're right on both accounts. Getting back to the fort's history… General Nelson A. Miles used the fort as his headquarters in his war against Geronimo in 1886. Even after the famous Indian surrendered, and the Apache threat was extinguished, the Army continued to operate the fort because of its strategic border position with Mexico. In 1913, it became the base for the Buffalo Soldiers of the 10th Cavalry Regiment, which was composed of Blacks. This was their base for nearly twenty years. For two years, 1916 – 1917, it was the headquarters for General John J. Pershing's failed "punitive expedition" to capture Poncho Villa, the Mexican nationalist who had raised hell along the border. During this period, the fort was commanded by Charles Young, the first Negro to be promoted to colonel."

"I never knew anything about this fellow Young. I'll put one of my more ambitious grad students on his trail tomorrow. So, please continue."

"In 1943, the base was home to the Black 92nd and 93rd Divisions. From their ranks, Major Holman hoped to find twenty volunteers, enlisted men who would make up the "initial test platoon." Ultimately, 16 men would come from the 92nd Division, along with three of its original six officers. In quick order the volunteers were transferred to Fort Benning, beginning on December 20, 1943. Unknown to the youthful recruits, the Army had issued orders authorizing the formation of the 555th Test Platoon one month earlier. Ten days later --- on December 30, 1943 --- the 555th Parachute Infantry Company was activated. At the time, no one fully realized that this represented a new chapter in American military history, one that would "help to change the social consciousness of white America and how Negroes were utilized in the Army.""

THE FIRST VOLUNTEERS

"Who were the first volunteers handpicked by Major Hoover? Those who have researched the question considered the recruits for the test platoon "some of the most intelligent and physically able men in the Army" at the time. Most had already received tough infantry training in the desert of Arizona. Most had endured the forced marches and steep climbs in the heat of Fort Huachuca sweltering sands and sharp-peaked mountains. Some were former university students. A few were ex-professional athletes, mainly from the Negro baseball leagues of the day. All were physically fit. On some level, each volunteer was highly motivated to make the program work. They all had something to prove.

MEANWHILE - WASHINGTON D.C.

The three old men departed their taxi in their area s of town, where Blacks could find accommodations, whether to rent or buy. Though the nation's capital, Washington D.C. was a southern town, segregated along racial lines, and beyond the gleaming monuments to Lincoln, Washington, and Jefferson, still an area imbued with the residue of "Jumping Jim Crow." Saying "good morning" to each other, they trailed off in different directions, each bearing with him the hope their morning excursion into the heart of the white power structure would be fruitful. It was now up to the White House and its cocktail-drinking, chain-smoking occupant to start the ball rolling. They could only hope.

CHAPTER 11

TRAINING

<u>1943 – FORT BENNING</u>

Garvey continued.

"The volunteers were immediately thrown into a rigorous training program. If they were to be paratroopers, the first such Negro outfit, they would have to pass muster. There would be no easy road.

"Training… That's what the Army called it. Do this. Do that. Do it this way. Do it that way.

"Becoming a paratrooper demanded the most rigorous training. Some would have suggested ruthless training. But it was necessary. Once you stepped out of a C-47, there was no turning back. Either you knew what to do or you didn't. There was no middle ground. You either floated to the ground, a billowing gown of nylon having brought you gently to "mother earth," or you plunged headlong into the unforgiving land, another casualty of an inadequate use of the chute. It was an all or nothing proposition.

"Over a four-week period the training was conducted in four stages to physically prepare the volunteers and to teach them all the skills necessary for their survival. It was not unlike the training undertaken by submarine crews. It was just that one group was headed for the ocean's depths, while the other sought the clouds above.

"The trainers were all white. Some were fair-minded and gave the Black recruits an even break. Others wanted them to fail, though they seldom voiced the view outright. It was rumored, however, that a betting pool had been set up by the jump-trainers, men mainly from the South. The bet was whether the volunteers would actually make their first jump. The big money bet against the Negro recruits."

"Betting against your trainees… That's malarkey."

"Malarkey, Professor?"

"Stupid stuff."

"I'll keep that in mind when my dad gets on my case."

"Prudently, I trust. Now… Back to Fort Benning."

———————

"The initial stage of training --- **A-Stage** --- was designed to put the men into the best possible physical shape. Three other things were also taught.

How to: (a) take care of their equipment; (b) exit an airplane through a mock door; and (c) collapse a parachute dragging across the ground.

TRAINING

"**B-Stage** training prepared the men for jumping by suspending them in a parachute harness before they jumped from a thirty-four foot tower, which tested their nerves as well as their ability to execute the jump commands.

"Jump commands, learn them, and execute them. They had to be programmed into the trainees until their responses were almost automatic. And there were lots of them to learn: "stand up," "hook up," "check equipment," sound off for equipment check," "stand in the door," and "ready to go."

SIMULATED JUMP

"**C-Stage** was a killer. It was advanced training. It consisted of parachuting from a 250-foot control tower and a 250-foot fire tower. The betting among the trainers increased with these jumps. The descent from these towers allowed a man to control the parachute and practice moves for maneuvering the parachute. If you didn't pass C-Stage, you washed out. There would be no D-Stage. All the volunteers passed.

PARACHUTE TRAINING TOWER

"**D-Stage** demanded that the men use all the skills they had been taught and a new one. They learned how to pack parachutes. Then they learned they would make five jumps from an airplane, four during the day, and one at night. The jumps were required. Without question, this was the most dangerous stage."

REQUIRED JUMPS

LATE 1943 – GREAT SMOKEY MOUNTAINS

Judge William Hastie looked up at the night sky. How beautiful the sparkling stars above, heavenly bodies not often seen from the bright lights of Washington, but so very apparent in the Great Smokey Mountains, where he had rented a cabin. Somewhere he hoped, at some time in the future, gallant young Negros would stare into the night sky as he was. Catching their breath and squeezing their jump cord they would make history if a benevolent God permitted that day had to come...

––––––––––––––––

JANUARY 24, 1944

Sixteen Negro men from the test platoon were loaded onto a C-47. You could cut the tenseness in the plane with the proverbial knife. The men were about to make a final practice jump. Thirty minutes later the plane reached jump altitude. A spotter plane flew on the right wing of the C-47. The jump would be photographed. History was being made, if the men jumped. It would be recorded. One of the first out the door was SGT Clarence H. Beavers. One of the last out was 1SGT Walter J. Morris. All the volunteers made their jump. No fatalities. No injuries. But there were lots of losers in the betting pool. The training had paid off."

PREPARING TO BOARD

"The last of the four jumps was completed on January 31, 1944. The next day the Negro paratroopers were presented their "parachute wings" for successfully completing their training. These men were the first Black paratroopers in the U.S. Army."

FEBRUARY 1944

Somewhere in Washington three older men smiled. Word had come to them through the city's grapevine. The 555th Airborne was a reality.

"Quite a story, Garvey."

"Isn't, mom?"

"Great job, son."

"Thanks, dad, but I can't take all the credit. Remember, Gramps gave me his notes, disarranged as they were. He's the guy who did the initial research. I'm sort of standing on his shoulders."

"I wonder why he never wrote them up," Professor Richmond added, "he certainly was on to something. I wonder."

"Professor?"

"I think we're two peas in the pod, your Gramps and myself. He was waiting for a grandson to take on the challenge, just as I've been holding my breath in hopes of finding a young historian to continue my work. It seems that, at least for the moment, both of us have found gold. Wonderful work, Garvey."

CHAPTER 12

TESTIMONY

"Garvey, surely you've heard of Thurgood Marshall and Hattie McDaniel?"

"Of course, Professor Richmond. And Joe Lewis and Jesse Owens, I heard about them too. And Jackie Robinson, you bet. Trailblazers, each and every one of them, I've been told. But not this guy, Walter Morris, at least until Gramps put me on his trail…"

"Your grandfather, why do I have the feeling he's always one large step ahead of us?"

"Us?"

"Well, we're in this together, aren't we?

"I guess so, Professor."

It was more than a guess. Garvey had been spending considerable time with Professor Richmond. He liked being on the U.W. campus. He liked being treated like an adult. He liked his research being taken seriously. High school was okay, social life, football games, cute girls, and his close buddies. But, as he knew, he was growing out of the regimented high school scene. Even with his college-prep classes, he was bored. Truth be told, he was ready for something more. This research project was giving him that chance, first with Gramps as a provocateur, and now with Professor Richmond as his mentor. Gramps pushed and prodded with cues and clues, while the good professor demanded multiple sources, careful analysis imbued with rigorous, painstaking concern for details. To Garvey's surprise, he took to this like that famous duck to water. Maybe, he thought on more than one occasion, this is what I'm cut out to do.

"Garvey, how did you come across the recording?"

"I wrote to his family."

"You wrote to Walter Morris' family? That simple?"

"Three letters. It took some time, back and forth, until they felt I was legit, that I could be trusted."

"You accomplished that how?"

"Just told them I was a high school student doing a research paper."

"Nothing else?"

"I told them I wanted to do right by Mr. Morris."

"You had a clincher?"

"I wanted his side of the story told."

"Born salesperson, Garvey."

"That's when they told me about the recording. I assume Morris wanted to write a book. Never got around to it. Figured it would help to record his thoughts. Leave something for his family. But I think it goes deeper."

"Explain."

"I don't think he wanted to disappear into history. He wanted the 555th to be remembered. He wanted to be remembered."

"An old-reel- to reel recording?"

"About the oldest technology, short of painting on cave walls, or marking wet clay that I know about, Professor Richmond."

"Or chiseling hard stone inside the Pyramids."

Garvey and his mentor laughed. But it wasn't the laughter of something funny. It was more like the wail of the past, crying out to be heard, asking not to be brushed aside. On that reel was history, a voice from the past trying once more to recapture a year and a half of pride and self-respect at a time of Jumping Jim Crow. The reel was no trifling artifact of an earlier time. It was more than that. It was Walter Morris seeking redemption, a lone figure screaming to the heavens, "I was once a soldier, a member of the Triple Nickles, a paratrooper."

THE TRIPLE NICKLES

"Fortunately, we have his recording, Professor."

"And thankfully, my good friend, Willie Simpson, was able to restore the reel. Not clear as a bell, but a darn sight better than when we first listened. The tape was so scratchy. Another few years and it would have deteriorated beyond repair. Always good to have a friend in the Drama Department with loads of electronic equipment and an old, still functioning reel-to-reel player. We've got a pretty clean copy now."

"I can't wait to listen."

"Lets. One little click..."

"And we're back in 1943."

————————

My name is Walter Morris. If you're not a member of my family you've probably never heard of me. That's okay. That's the way the War Department wanted it back in late 1943, and for the next two years. Especially 1945... You may have heard of the 555th Airborne, but not the top-secret mission the group was involved in as the war in the Pacific was coming to an end. The government didn't talk about it. We couldn't talk about it. Not during the war or after it for many years... That is, until now. Finally, I can tell you what happened.

WALTER MORRIS

Let's start at the beginning. It was 1940... I decided to join the Army. It was shortly before Pearl Harbor. In those days, I wasn't called a Black, Negro, or African-American. I was called "colored." Because of this, I was treated like most other colored persons in America. The country, all too often in many places, was racist. The Army certainly was a racist outfit back then. Oh, not all enlistees or officers, but a majority... That was for sure at Fort Benning in Georgia and elsewhere, especially in the South. I was treated like a servant in the Army. I could be a cook. I could guard facilities. I could drive a truck. I could load the ships. I could do mess hall duty. When trained I got the oldest equipment. If barracked I slept in the building closest to falling down. It was overt racism. I felt unwanted. Undesired. And certainly misunderstood... Daily acts of humiliation can get to a guy. It got to me. You begin to believe what others are saying about you. You get an inferiority complex. After a while, you know you're a "second class citizen." That's the way you feel.

I wanted to prove myself. I washed out of officer training. The system rejected me. Just spit me out of officer's club. Negroes need not apply. Same old stuff I experienced when looking for a civilian job. But I had leadership qualities. Others knew that. I knew. I pushed hard. In time I became a non-commissioned officer. Wartime needs hurried up promotions, even when colored men were involved.

You would think a uniform would win you points. On the dance floor with a pretty girl most probably... In a photograph sent home to your parents, no question about it... But not always, even when you become, as I did, the first colored officer to earn the coveted U.S. Airborne Parachutist badge --- my wings.

A couple of examples come to mind. I was in a train station in North Carolina, a commissioned officer, wearing my paratrooper uniform when two burly M.P.'s ask me to show "proof of my military status." I quickly showed them my printed orders. Instead of accepting them --- and me --- they said the orders were insufficient. I could, they said, be impersonating a paratrooper. Why I would want to do that, they never explained. They just arrested me. It was only after an officer checked that I was released. I never forgot that humiliating episode. But it taught me a good lesson. Whether peacetime or wartime, prejudice doesn't discriminate. Biases are equal opportunity devils.

Eating time at Fort Benning was the worst... Again, even for an officer. White trainees came in the front door of the mess hall and went to a counter for their food. The colored soldiers were told to come in through a side door and went to their immediate right to the first available table, which was always available, it seemed, for them. We were not permitted to go to the counter. Our food was brought to us by other colored soldiers. I don't remember being waited on by a white soldier. We left by the side door after eating. The white solders went out the front door.

I heard stories that really jacked me up. On one occasion, Black soldiers in South Carolina stopped at a diner for lunch. The owner refused to serve the soldiers inside. Instead, he brought out lunches in brown bags. If the black soldiers needed to use the restrooms, they couldn't go inside. Outside was a separate privy for colored soldiers. As bad as that was, the worst was still to come. Inside the diner were German POW's enjoying their meal and smoking cigarettes. They grinned at the colored soldiers, *as almost to say, "I may be a Nazi, a POW, but I'm white. I get to eat inside." Captured in Europe or North Africa, the POW's were brought to the U.S. to do agricultural work. Stories like this made me angry. They made everybody angry. But what could anyone do? The German POW's pulled rank.*

I was determined, if the opportunity arose, to make amend for these slights. I absolutely refused to see myself as less able than a white soldier. I fought back against the inferiority complex afflicting so many young Blacks. I kept thinking of myself as a "first class citizen." I wasn't going to let the boss man get to me.

At Fort Benning I was the sergeant for a unit of colored soldiers. That's where the Army was training white soldiers to be parachutists. The basic training took place between 8 a.m. and 4:00 p.m. During that period, colored soldiers did guard duty for the most part. It was a perfectly stifling job. Stand here. Walk there. Talk about boring. Though they had been well trained at Fort Huachuca before they came to Benning the men under me soon lacked discipline and any sense of purpose. Fighting Hitler and the Emperor by shoveling manure in Georgia didn't turn a man on. Morale was in the pits, about six feet below any hole you could conjure up. They were beginning to act the way white officers said they would and in many cases hoped they would --- like "colored soldiers." I knew I had to change all this. I began with the baseplate.

———————————

"What's a baseplate?"

"Very old term, Garvey. You'd know it if you were in the Army."

"It refers to what?"

"It's the baseplate of an 81 millimeter mortar. Quite heavy. Needs to handle the impact of the mortar firing. It absorbs the recoil. Sort of like a shield."

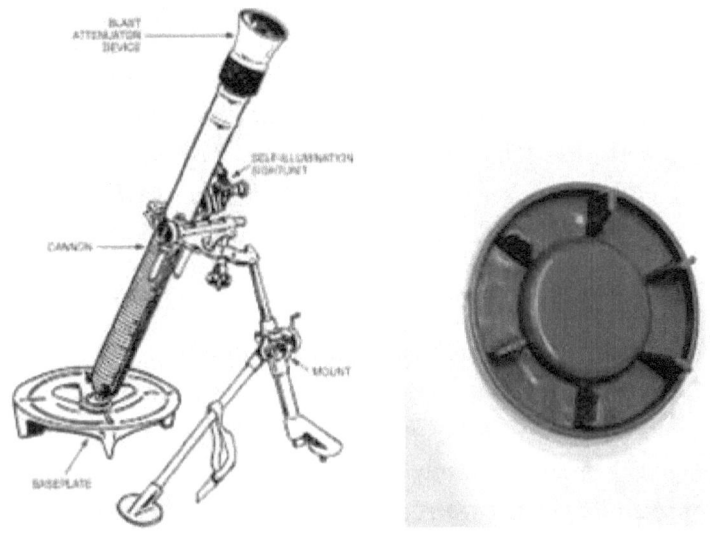

BASEPLATE

"Why would Morris start with that?"

———————

It was customary for colored soldiers to greet each other as if they were at home, using the street language of their former communities. They might say to a friend at the mess hall door, "You can go in first, %$#&*." It was not said in anger. More like a habit, but it lacked style. I decided to stop this. Language is important. It tells a lot about a man. Appropriate words suggests discipline and pride... Good morale... Any man uttering &%$#@*& had to carry a baseplate on his back as he walked around the company area. That was his punishment. It was kind of like a "scarlet letter," only on the outside for the whole world to see. It marked you as a jerk. Soon the men got the idea. Knock off the %^$#*&. Act like soldiers. With a wide grin, my men at times said, "Good morning, baseplate" to each other. It was a start.

More needed to be done; I was sure of that. In time a plan emerged in my mind. No grand design and certainly a little unfocused. It had come to me as I watched the white soldiers training. Soon I knew their training practices. I memorized their routine. I figured I could duplicate their practices with my guys when the practices fields were unoccupied. I took my plan to the commanding officer. He begrudgingly said, "Ok." His heart wasn't in it, one way or the other. Actually, I think, he "couldn't cared less" about what I did. No one on the base, it seemed, cared about the Negro soldier in the "service company." As long as we did our job in the day, the view was, "What difference could it really make whatever we did on our own time?"

On the calisthenics field the men got into shape. I saw to that. I worked them hard. I pushed them. We also emulated the white troops, jumping from a five-foot platform into a pit. We did everything except jump from a 250-tower or a plane in flight. We would even sit in a replica of a C-47 pretending to be paratroopers, two long rows of soldiers caught up in a fantasy world where men are treated equally and fairly.

An idea was beginning to take shape. Negroes could do anything a white soldier did. All they needed was the opportunity. The men began to carry themselves differently. Within weeks, they wore shined shoes, and pressed their clothes. Their hair was cut and combed. Their morale improved. They realized they were "just as good as the white students; no better but no worse." Still something more was needed. We had to get on the tower. We had to get into a flying C-47. Just how many times can you leap off a five-foot deck? We needed a break.

One day, while doing our routine, our "pretend colored paratroopers" were observed by the new company commander, General Ridgley Gaither. He was a Southerner. He knew the world of Jim Crow. He had a reputation of "being as tough as nails and just as straight." I really didn't expect any support from him. How wrong I was.

Unknown to me, he had been watching my practices, pretend or otherwise. He was impressed by the performance of the men. One day he called me into his office. I was nervous as hell as I went to see him. I fully expected to be reprimanded for some infraction or, worst of all, told *to stop the shadow paratrooper practices. Once more, how wrong my thinking proved to be.*

Gaither told me about a highly classified decision recently made in Washington. The order had gone out to create a company comprised solely of colored soldiers or as the order read, "all Colored troops." I was floored. He then asked me to accept the position of First Sergeant of the Company. Floored again... I accepted.

Years later I learned how all this happened. President Roosevelt had been pressured by A. Philip Randolph and Roy Wilkins, plus General Benjamin O. Davis to desegregate the armed forces and, short of this, to establish a Negro airborne company. Randolph represented the unions. Wilkins was a political organizer in the Negro community. General Davis was the first Black general of that rank. But what really convinced the President to act was the threat of a massive "march on Washington" to "dramatize the need for more jobs in the defense plants and to accept colored men in the Parachute School." This was, of course, twenty years before Martin Luther King's famous speech during a later "march on Washington." As history would have it, A. Philip Randolph was to organize the first march, which never happened, and did organize the second, which actually occurred.

There were, as one might expect, plenty of doubters. Many felt that colored men would never jump out of a plane. Indeed, many wanted us to fail. It was rank prejudice. The same sort of attitude about the Japanese before Pearl Harbor --- "slanted-eyed people couldn't fly airplanes." Or the Russian peasant army --- "Hitler's hoards will run all over them." Or the Nisei in California --- "Japanese-Americans can't be trusted. Place them in relocation camps." And so it went. Stereotypes created to comfort the biased only to be proven wrong. Pearl Harbor attested to Japanese eyesight. The defense of Moscow proved the worth of the Soviet soldier. As to the Japanese-Americans, there was not one known incident of sabotage during the war. Those in the military served honorably.

It was my task to get volunteers. I had to find the right men to make this experiment work. Fort Huachuca was the answer. Lots of well-trained Negro soldiers were there. Surely, there would be volunteers there for the chance to be in the Airborne. And, of course, there were. The Buffalo Soldiers were once from the same garrison following the Civil War. Our future paratroopers were from there, too. To honor the Buffalo Soldiers, we decided to call ourselves the "Triple Nickles," even purposely misspelling he name to bring attention to ourselves. We really did know how to spell nickel, though some suggested otherwise. And that's the way the "buffalo nickel" got into history, at least as far as the 555th was concerned.

We had a name. We were finally getting the training. All we needed was a mission.

––––––––––––––––

"They never got a mission, did they, Professor Richmond?"

"Wrong, Garvey."

"I can't find any mention of one. Not in the European theater, not in the Pacific."

"Doesn't mean they didn't have one, does it?"

"The top-secret something Morris was talking about?"

"Must be?"

"You know what it was, Professor?"

"I do."

"Well?"

"Something that didn't demand the mixing of white and colored soldiers, if you can believe that."

"Combat?"

"In a way, yes."

"Against a fierce enemy?"

"Who took no quarter."

"Against the Russians?"

"No."

"Well, if the 555th had a mission, it had to be against someone!"

"Absolutely, Garvey, or something."

"I'm puzzled."

"Understandable. Hint, it had to do indirectly with something that General Mark Clark said about the 555th. He considered the group a "social experiment." Commenting, he said, "We have a war to fight and win. I don't need the added war that would be fought between our own men if I have to integrate the soldiers.""

"Crap."

"Beats your WOW. And it was, as you say, crap." But Clark had a point Defeating Berlin and Tokyo was the key to everything. No Blacks would storm either city. No white lives would be saved by the courage and death of a Black soldier. Whites would perish on the beaches of Normandy and in the waters offshore at Okinawa. For the most part, Black soldiers would be bystanders. For the Pentagon, integration was a side issue except to Black soldiers."

"Doesn't seem right."

"Garvey, bless your heart, you're an idealist. In this old world of ours, unfairness is the rule, not the exception. The only question concerns the degree of unfairness and, when it happens to you, how you'll respond. This was the challenge before Walter Morris. The injustices could not be swept away. He didn't have a broom that large. All he could do was be ready. Keep his men honed to the highest skill level. And hope... Hope that something would change Washington's mind. Hope that his men would have at least one opportunity to show their mettle. Hope that something would occur that would bypass Clark's rejection of the 555th. That's all Walter Morris could do."

"Something came along?"

"Oh, yes. But here's the paradox. Almost no one would know about it, or how the 555th was used to meet a threat unanticipated by the Pentagon."

"Which was?"

"A balloon, Garvey. A very big balloon."

CHAPTER 13

BALLOON BOMBS

<u>2028 – NEAR MOSES LAKE, WASHINGTON</u>

"Are we there yet?" Garvey asked, not with the impatience of a third-grader, but rather with the restlessness of an adolescent detective on the hunt. "We've been on the road at least four hours."

"Closer to five," his father replied, a smile shimmering on his face. "Recall we had a slight delay getting started this morning."

"Those women," Gramps said begrudgingly in a way that was more pretense than actual upset. "If they had just left us alone."

Garvey's father couldn't help but chuckle. Gramps was right. The women had been on their case. Do this. Don't do that. What did you forget? Silly sort of question, don't you think? If you knew what you forgot it wouldn't be forgotten. Then the health questions: My medication? The new breath-inhaler for Garvey, did he take it? And Gramps' motley group of senior citizen medicines guaranteed to keep you alive unless you died? Then came the fiscal inquisition. "Matt, did you take your credit cards?" his wife, Blair, asked three times. Do you have enough cash?" Finally, the geography-related question... The next generation Apple navigation software, did you upload it?" On and on it went, insatiable edicts, concerns, and female sage wisdom. God, how their spouses could interrogate.... I guess that's what happens when a 16-year old joins his father, approaching 54-years, and an old guy staring

90-years in the face, on a trip across the state in what could be called a spur of the moment decision.

"Is this trip necessary?" Garvey's mother had asked before her husband pressed the ignition button.

"Absolutely" responded his father. "Gramps flew up here for this."

"Gramps put you up to this," she quickly added, an accusatory tone to her voice. "I know he's behind all this business with the 555th. And now he's got you involved."

"Blair, I read Garvey's research notes and his draft copy. He's done a great job. And, yes, I'm hooked. I want to know how the story will turn out."

"You should read it, daughter-in-law. The kid has talent."

"You instigator, Gramps," Blair quickly said in response. "You just want to get out on the open road. That's why you forced my husband along," she continued. "You can't drive."

"I can drive," Gramps said, "just not too far from the house. That's where Grandma comes in. Fewer restrictions on her license."

"Better eye sight and coordination," Grandma spoke up for the first time. "And I didn't miss any of the written questions unlike someone else I know."

"Better eye sight, who are you kidding? You were flirting with the examiner. Fluttering your eyelashes, inhaling deeply. The poor guy never had a chance."

"Jealous?"

"Of your fewer restrictions, yes."

What could the two women do? Blair knew there was no way to stop this trip. Her son was being hijacked. These guys were on a quest and he was going along with obvious glee. If only Garvey's AP history teacher hadn't assigned a research paper. If only Garvey hadn't asked his grandfather for a possible topic. If only her husband hadn't introduced Garvey to Professor Richmond. If only the good Professor hadn't contacted some guy in the middle of the state. If only this mysterious person hadn't invited them to his home. If all these "if" moments hadn't occurred… It was enough to make you believe in karma. Three generations were about to hit the road. Whatever was going on was beyond her. But secretly, she wanted them to have a good time. And unbeknownst to her husband she had read some of Garvey's research. Her son had talent. She had complimented him with pride. Still, she wished he wasn't headed to Moses Lake.

As for Grandma… She just smiled. No sense fighting city hall. Fate had taken hold of these three. Out there, down the road answers awaited them. Like marooned men in the desert they were thirsty for answers. As for her husband… Well, the old guy wanted one more bite of the apple. That was obvious. Considering his age his health was okay. Twelve pills each day kept the mortician at bay. After being married to him for almost 60 years, she knew all his tricks. He had taken Garvey's simple query about a topic and run with it. From the very beginning, he's been pulling strings, manipulating events, pushing Garvey. Somehow he was living vicariously through the young man as they plunged ahead, unearthing the previously unknown, ferreting out what had happened as they peeled back the onionskins of the past. Yet, a little voice told her there was something else in play, something more to the whole story, something tied to her husband, some unfinished business. As to what it was, she had no idea. Well, "rah" for the old guy. Go for it. Give father time a big kick in the rump. Have your date with history and make peace with the past. But just don't teach Garvey too many swear words.

"Who is this guy again, Gramps? The man we're visiting."

"Thomas Sprague, Junior?"

"Who is he?"

"He took a class with Professor Richmond a few years ago, Garvey. He's a real history buff, especially World War II. They swapped a lot of stories. Through the young man, Richmond met Thomas' father, Thomas senior. He had been an FBI agent during the war. Attached to the San Francisco branch. He was part of the investigation of the 'sightings' in late 1944 and most of '45. He was the FBI liaison with the Army. That got him involved with Project Fire-Fly. That's when the Professor learned about what's in the barn."

"That's why we're going to Moses Lake?" Garvey asked. "To learn how all of this is related to the 555th?"

"You catch on quick," Gramps replied with a big smile.

"Actually, just outside of Moses Lake, "Garvey's dad added, on the outskirts of Moses Lake State Park. That's where we turn off for the Sprague farm."

"What's in the barn, Gramps?"

"The key to everything."

"Teasing me again?"

"I already gave you the answer, sort of, before we left. Remember I told you to check out that old movie."

"*Independence Day?*"

"Made in 1996."

"I saw it."

"Okay, Garvey," his father interrupted, "what's the big scene in the movie?"

"Destroying the mother ship and the aliens?"

"No."

"Knocking out an alien fighter in the desert?"

"Nope."

"Watching the capital go up in flames?"

"A good choice, but no. Think about the barn."

"There was no barn in the film."

"Symbolically, Garvey," Gramps said.

"The secret base in New Mexico? Near Roswell? Area 51?"

"Keep going. What did the President and his aides see in the hidden complex?"

"An alien space ship. A fighter from the mother ship."

"Bingo."

"That's what we're going to see, Gramps? Aliens?"

"Sort of. Do you remember the response of the President in the movie?"

"Disbelief. Astonishment. He was stunned."

"Well, get ready for a repeat."

At Coulee City, where US 2 intersected with State 17, Garvey's dad turned southward. They drove past Sur Lakes State Park, then the Lake Lenore Caves, before passing through Lakeview Park. Lot of Lakes in this part of Washington State. About five miles north of Moses Lake, they turned right onto a two-lane county road. They passed a number ranches and farms, seeing on more than one occasion the ubiquitous John Deere tractor in the fields. Finally, they came across a battered old sign reading, "*Sprague Farm.*" Here they turned in, traveling along a gravel road until they saw the farm house and adjacent to it, standing wide and cavernous, an oversize wooden barn, seemingly forlorn in the late afternoon sun, as if it was still in mourning for some lost cause. A sense of sadness pervaded the structure, uninviting, yet beckoning as if it couldn't make up its mind. And its size, you could park the Goodyear blimp in it or so it seemed. As they parked, a tall, rather thin man came out of the farmhouse, a slight smile on his face. He appeared to be in his mid-forties. He was wearing a uniform designating him a Washington State Park Ranger.

"You fellas made it. Come on in. Bring your stuff. There's lots of room in the old place. We'll have a bite, then visit the barn."

An hour later --- after introductory jabber --- and after some pretty good cheddar cheese and salami sandwiches, brewed hot coffee, and wedges of apple pie, the group approached the barn. Garvey, of course, had had a glass of milk almost straight from the cow, and a sizeable helping of vanilla ice cream with his pie. Oh, the young... They had stomachs of wrought iron with a corresponding appetite or so it seemed. The older men could only look on with a mixture of disgust and envy.

"Garvey, I bet you're not ready for what you're going to see."
"Probably not, Mr. Sprague. Of course, I'm completely in the dark. My dad and Gramps keep hinting about it, whatever 'it' is, saying it has something to do with the 555th."

"You bet. That's why Professor Richmond contacted me. Mentioned your name Garvey and what you're up to. No way I could not invite you. Darn few people seem interested in this piece of history today."

"We are," Garvey's Dad said with the authority of a school administrator. Not at first, however, at least on my part. But after I reviewed my son's research. I was caught, hook, line, and sinker."

"Took you awhile," Gramps added.

"Didn't figure, though, you guys would come so quickly."

"Missing two days of school for this," Garvey said somewhat shyly. "Was my mother ticked!"

"Well, another school is about to open," the younger Sprague rejoined quickly. "The barn awaits."

Sprague Junior unlocked the three heavy, rusted locks holding the barn doors securely closed. Whatever was inside, he didn't want disturbed. He went inside, and a moment later very dim lights kicked on. Sprague waved the guys inside. Then they saw it.

THE FORGOTTEN BALLOON BOMB

The balloon was startling large, well over 35-feet in diameter. It was 70 feet long from the balloon's top to the odd metal basket below. It took up almost all the space in the barn. In the shadowy light it looked like a giant mothball peering down at them. Though tethered to a large cast-iron anvil, the balloon still moved, drifting a few feet in all directions because of air movement within the immense barn. Large stains on the balloon bag seem to give it facial features. As you walked near it, it seemed to watch you. The slightest movement of the balloon was eerie and certainly frightening if one let his imagination romp. All in all, there was something menacing about it.

"Was it worth the trip?" Sprague asked.

"Jesus," Matt said. "Look at the size of that thing!"

"I never realized they were this large," Gramps said. "How the hell did you get it into the barn?"

"In due time all questions will be answered. What about you, Garvey? Cat got your tongue?

"You're sure this isn't Area 51?"

Garvey peered intently at the balloon. He saw that it was connected by a series of ropes and heavy wire to a circular-like object to which a series of sandbags were attached. It wasn't a basket in the usual sense. There was no real room for a person. He also saw four metal objects, neatly polished and somehow deadly in their apparent inertness. The metal contraption moved a little in harmony with the air bag above.

THE DEADLY BASKET

Sprague interrupted Garvey's concentration, saying, "The balloon fabric was constructed by hundreds of Japanese high school girls from bits of a tough paper called washi, which was made from mulberry trees and glued together with potato paste. The use of this material, plus the concept of a balloon bomb was the brainchild of Major General Sueyoshi Kusaba of the Japanese Ninth Army Technical Research Laboratory. The project was code-named FUGO. That was an acronym meaning a "wind ship weapon.""

"High school girls?" asked Garvey's father, more than amazed by what he had heard.

"All sworn to secrecy. They couldn't even tell their parents what they were doing each day in the school. And they were watched by soldiers."

"Watched?"

"To make sure they were doing their job and that they weren't eating the glue."

"What?"

"It was near the end of the war. Food supplies were limited. The girls were on a near-starvation diet. The glue was appealing, just not nutritious."

"But why balloon bombs?" Garvey asked.

"The war in the Pacific, young man, was all but over except for the killing. Our B-29's were systematically firebombing Japanese cities, burning them to cinders. What was left of the Japanese air force could not stop this terror from the skies. Our navy had destroyed the once magnificent Japanese fleet, permitting us to blockade the country, and, if necessary, starve the population until the government capitulated. On all fronts the Japanese army was retreating --- China, Southeast Asia, Iwo Jima, and Okinawa. The balloon bomb was Japan's limited answer to all this, a way to attack the United States proper."

It was *Independence Day* all over for Garvey. He felt like the actor-President in the movie, amazed, surprised, overwhelmed. The "thing" might as well come from outer space. He half expected aliens to emerge from it. As he gazed stubbornly at the balloon, it hit him. This huge weapon was somehow a tangible connection to the 555th. Exactly how, he didn't know yet. That there was a connection he had no doubt.

"What you're looking at is a Japanese balloon bomb."
"How the hell did it get into your barn?" Gramps asked again.
"That's a story and a half."

"Back in 1944 my father was with the FBI. Working with the Army and local law enforcement, it was his job to locate these Japanese-fashioned weapons before they started forest fires, damaged military installations, or killed someone. Many thousands of these babies were launched by Japan, beginning in 1944. They traveled across the Pacific, pushed by the jet stream at about 30,000 feet. This prevailing air current moved from west to east. Perfect for what they Japanese had in mind. The balloons were filled with hydrogen. That's what's in this one. Got my own small supply for special occasions. Don't ask how I do this. Anyway, by the 5th of August 1945, the balloon attack tapered off. About that time, my father heard about a sighting in what's now the Moses Lake State Park, not far from here. He investigated. He got the surprise of his life. A balloon had landed in an open field undamaged. For whatever reason, its four incendiary bombs hadn't exploded. With the help of his FBI team, local police, and a few strong farm hands, the bombs were dismantled --- that is, disarmed, and the hydrogen was released from the balloon bag. The whole contraption was brought by truck to this barn for storage until the Army came to check it out."

"And?"

"Garvey, that never happened. The next day the *Enola Gay* dropped an atomic bomb on Hiroshima. Two days later, another bomb leveled Nagasaki. That's what made the headlines. The war was over. The boys were coming home. Celebrations everywhere. What was in the barn was forgotten. It just slipped through the government's bureaucratic fingers. No one came for it. And my dad didn't say anything. After a while, except for our family, the balloon disappeared into history. My father cared for it like an old car. Don't ask me why. For some reason he felt an attachment to it. After his death, I continued to look after it. After I'm gone, I don't know. Anyway check out this diagram. It partially explains what you're looking at."

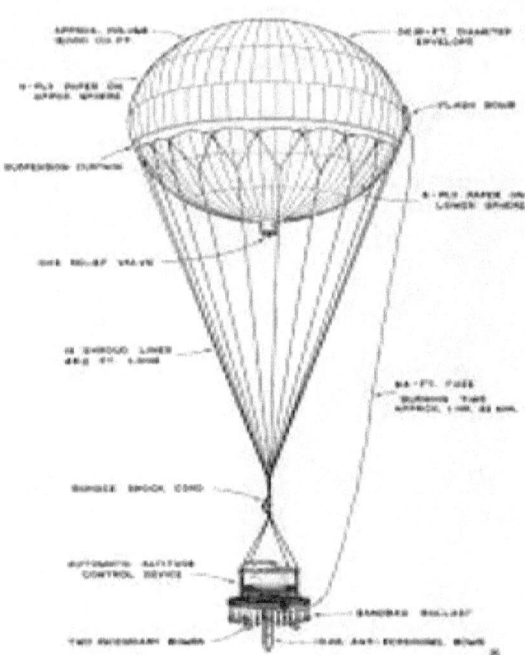

"See those sandbags. Took time to find them. Each time a balloon descended below 25,000 feet from the loss of gas, a "barometric pressure switch automatically dropped a sandbag." Naturally, this caused the balloon to rise again toward the 30,000-foot level. These balloons traveled, believe it or not, up to 125 miles an hour. After leaving Japan, it took them from 80 to 120 hours to reach the West Coast of the United States. Everything depended on the winds and, of course, the weather. If the Japanese had calculated correctly, the last sandbag was dropped after the balloon crossed into American airspace. At that point a second automatic switch took over as the balloon descended to 27,000 feet. The switch released the bombs. Once the last bomb was dropped a fuse was ignited automatically that set off a demolition charge, which destroyed the balloon. In the case of this balloon the bombs weren't dropped and the charge didn't go off. That's why the balloon was found intact."

BALLOON BOMB

"The balloon bombs were called *"fusen bakudan."* All together over 9,000 of them were launched from the Japanese island of Honshu. About 300 or more made it to the U.S. But the number could be as high as 900. To be more exact, 342 were either sighted or found. Many authorities contend that balloon bombs, unknown to us, still lie unexploded in wilderness areas. In fact, the most recent discovery of one was in 1992, 47-years after the war ended."

"One question, Mr. Sprague," Garvey said perhaps a little too loudly. "Did the Japanese really think these balloon bombs would win the war?"

"Good question young man. No, of course not. Irritate us, yes. Cause some confusion, certainly, but change the course of the war, not in a million years."

"So why did they launch them?"

"Try to understand the Japanese situation in late 1944. As I said before, their navy had suffered a number of catastrophic defeats. The Imperial navy was no more. Japanese naval aviation was all but destroyed. Pilots, planes, and aircraft carriers were gone. In China she was caught up in a bloody stalemate with the Chinese government in a war that began in 1933. On one Pacific high-defended island after another American Marines were advancing triumphantly across the vast stretches of Magellan's lake. The Philippines were falling to MacArthur's troops. Iwo Jima and Okinawa were looming American targets. And in the air, the Boeing B-29's were devastating Japanese cities. Literally burning them to the ground... The Russians were beginning to mass troops on the Manchurian border in preparation for an advance into Manchuria and then into Korea before attacking Japan. In Europe the Nazi armies were retreating on all fronts. Japan's ally was sandwiched between Eisenhower's troops in the west and Stalin's armies in the east. There was no good news. Defeat of the Empire was imminent. It was just a matter of how many more Japanese and Americans would die before General Tojo's government surrendered. The Japanese were desperate."

"But why balloon bombs?" Garvey again asked.

"It was a weapon of last resort and, believe it or not, the world's first intercontinental weapon, traveling even greater distances than the German V-I and V-2 rockets. In short, the Japanese struck back where they could with what they could. It was as simple as that."

"You mentioned 'sightings,' Garvey's Dad said, interrupting Sprague. "What can you tell us about them?"

"Let's go back into the house. Lots to talk about."

CHAPTER 14

ARRIVAL

Sprague continued:

"On August 18, 1945, the *Seattle Times,* our largest state newspaper, now freed of government censorship following Japan's surrender, revealed the "balloon story" to its readers. The story enumerated the so-called balloon sightings. Those who read the article were amazed at what happened in their state in the last year of the war.

"On February 27, 1945, a balloon exploded in the air near Goldendale, Washington. The next day another one blew up 10 miles northwest of Tacoma. No one knew what caused the explosions. Plane crash… Natural gas pipe ruptured… Those were the usual explanations. Another balloon landed in Washington on a farm between Puyallup and Orting on March 3rd. In every case, the investigating officers, usually the FBI, swore witnesses to secrecy. Five balloons were spotted in Mount Rainer National Park. Park Rangers had been alerted to look for them. Another balloon landed on telephone wires near Bremerton. A telephone lineman, unsure what he was dealing with, cut down the balloon. Fortunately, he was not hurt. But it was a close call.

"The *Times* also reported "the highest number of balloons seen in one day in the state was 58." The article revealed that crews of B-29 planes flying westward toward Japan had "seen hundreds of balloons in the air on bombing missions." It was thought at first that the balloons were meant to be obstructions to the planes. Can you imagine it? Hundreds of B-29's flying westward over a sky full of balloons moving eastward. It must have been quite a sight. What the B-29 guys were seeing, as I said earlier, the first ICBM, the first unmanned missile flying between continents, though at a more modest speed.

"Two woodchoppers made history in December 1944. They discovered the first balloon bomb near Kalispell, Montana. Apparently, the bombs had been released automatically. No damage was done. On February 22, 1945, a Royal Canadian air force plane shot down a balloon. It was the first balloon destroyed in the air. The shoot down was only 20 miles north of Bellingham. American pilots were doing the same."

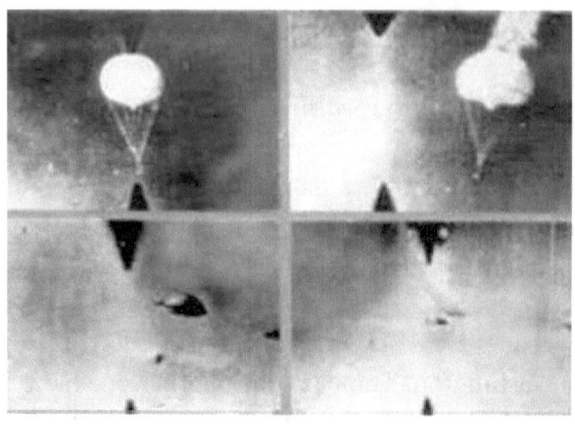

DOWNING A BALLOON BOMB

"There were some funny sighting-experiences, believe it or not. In Yakima, for example, a boy "unknowingly carried around a Jap anti-personnel bomb he found near his home." It had come from a balloon bomb. He did this for several days "before white-faced authorities persuaded him it was dangerous." The boy almost killed himself. He thought he was playing with a toy airplane. He wound the "propeller," the arming device in the nose of the weapon. If he had twisted the armed bomb's "detonating device 1/16th of an inch more it would have exploded."

"On another occasion, the children in an Indian family, after discovering a balloon, built a beautiful tepee from its fabric in their backyard. This was near Wapato, Washington. The kids were really hurt when the FBI snatched it away.

"Near Moxee, Washington, a sheepherder found a fallen balloon with live bombs. He dragged it behind his automobile and kept it in a building for two weeks before the local police found out. Talk about being lucky. A few of his sheepherder friends thought he was trying to pull the wool over the government.

"One balloon was reported to have landed on a turkey farm. The bombs didn't go off. No turkeys were killed. At least, not until Thanksgiving or so the story goes.

"Levity aside there was some serious moments. In 1945, as delegates were attending the first meeting of the United Nations in San Francisco, hundreds of balloons were reported at sea and heading toward the Golden Gate Bridge. Presumably they all crashed at sea, harmlessly and isolated from the city.

"In early 1945, a balloon bomb came down near the Hanford atomic bomb factory in south central Washington. Another one fell on power lines near Bonneville Dam, momentarily stopping power to the Hanford facility. The Hanford incident was a near calamity. The facility was "turning out uranium slugs for the atomic bomb that would destroy Nagasaki." The bomb was called "Fat Man." One of the balloon bombs became tangled in electrical transmission lines "causing a temporary short circuit in the power for the nuclear reactor cooling pumps." Fortunately, the backup safety devices restored power almost immediately. If they hadn't and the cooling system had been off a few minutes longer, a reactor might have collapsed or even exploded. This nightmare would have created the world's first Chernobyl. Radiation would have been released. "The havoc," according to nuclear experts, "would have been unimaginable." Because of the randomness of the jet stream, two-balloon bombs almost destroyed a $2,000,000,000 project that was essentially unknown to the Japanese military. Had the plant been destroyed no second bomb would have been available for months.

"Against infinitesimal odds and the capriciousness of nature, two balloon bombs had hit the most important target on the American mainland, short of the White House. And amazingly the Japanese would never know. Censorship cloaked all mention of the incident, as it did regarding other balloon bomb sightings. The free press was persuaded not to publish any news accounts. The Japanese were in the dark with respect to the effectiveness (or lack of) of their balloon campaign."

"At least no one was killed by the balloon bombs," Garvey said in a somewhat questioning manner."

"No members of the military. That's true."

"You're hedging your answer," Garvey's dad said quietly. "What about the civilian population?"

"Only one known incident, a very sad story. Retelling it is difficult for me. Stirs unhappy emotions."

"If you would rather not…"

"No, you need to know what happened. It may put things in perspective. The only known civilian fatalities caused by the balloon bombs occurred on May 5, 1945 near the small town of Bly, Oregon just north of the state line with California. A pregnant woman named Elsie Mitchell and five children from their local church were having a picnic before going fishing in the Fremont National Forest. Her husband, the Reverend Archie Mitchell, was parking the car after dropping off his wife and kids. One of the kids spotted a strange object dangling from a large balloon entrapped in the branches of a towering tree. The kids went to investigate, as did Mrs. Mitchell. As Mr. Mitchell saw them doing this he yelled out for them to stop. Apparently, he had some prior knowledge about the balloon bomb danger. His wife and children didn't hear him, or simply failed to heed his advice. When touched by one of the kids the object exploded, killing all the children and Mrs. Mitchell. The first news reports said the blast was of "unannounced cause."

"Poor kids," Gramps said.

"And the father was untouched?" Garvey's father asked.

"Parking the car. Not a scratch."

"The only civilians killed were mostly kids," Garvey said sadly. "Just kids."

"By coincidence," Sprague went on, "there was a road crew at work nearby led by Richard Barnhouse. He was operating a grader about 150-yards from the kids. He saw the children form a semi-circle around something. But from his vantage point, he couldn't see what they were looking at. Then there was an explosion. He ran to the children, finding them burned, mangled, and dead. None were conscious, including Mrs. Mitchell.

Apparently the balloon had been hanging in the trees for a month or more. That was indicted by the weathering and mildew on the fabric. Sadly, children found it, not adults until it was too late."

"Not fair," Garvey literally yelled out, his angry voice denoting an emotion he had never experienced before.

"The Japanese probably felt the same way when our bombs destroyed their families," Sprague added, a tragic sadness in his voice. "War spares no one."

"And the effort to keep everything secret?" Gramps asked. "Why the hush-hush?"

"The Bly Incident was kept secret from the American people, The Oregon Forestry Service played a strong role in doing this, as indicated in a letter from L.K. Mays, Forest Supervisor, to F.H. Armstrong, also known as Spike. In the letter, Mays compliments the District Manager for avoiding confusion and a panic in the area by keeping lid on the Bly story. This must have been painful for Spike since, according to Mays, he knew many of the children and certainly the Mitchells.

"Though not stated directly, Mays' letter recognized the need for secrecy demanded by the government concerning the balloon bombs. Lt. Col. Bisenius of the U.S. Army was also very complimentary of the manner in which the Forest Service handled this incident. He stated that this was the most prompt and effectively handled case they (the Army) had experienced. This was remarkable especially as the loss of six lives was involved.

"Secrecy was important. The Army didn't want the Bly incident made public. And with good reason… It didn't need a panic on the West Coast in the last days of the war. What the Army was really concerned with was a balloon bomb threat that never materialized. American officials were concerned that the Japanese would resort to biological warfare agents. It was feared the balloon might carry anthrax or other communicable diseases. Though it never happened, the fear was not unfounded. The Japanese began experiments in 1937 with chemical-biological agents. After the war, it was learned that these experiments included tests on prisoners of war in the 'notorious Unit 731.' Though nearing defeat in 1945, the Japanese government refused to permit biological warfare. Perhaps the government was fearful of reprisals."

"And what about those five kids?"

"Garvey, secrecy then but not now. Where the bomb exploded there is now a monument."

"Any questions, Garvey?" Sprague Junior asked.

" Couple of hundred."

"Garvey, how about one or two?"

"Okay. Why did the Japanese stop the balloon bomb campaign?"

"Good questions. First of all, they thought that no news meant there was no significant war damage. They hadn't considered the power of enforced censorship. What they didn't know did hurt them. Second, one intent of the attack was to start major forest fires in the Northwest.

Here climate and weather conspired against the Japanese. The best time for favorable high-altitude winds, the jet stream, was winter, which, of course, was the wet seasons, snow, rain, and ice in the Northwest. It's tough to start a forest fire at that time of the year regardless of your explosive. Third, American high-level carpet bombings by the B-29's had damaged Japanese industry, including hydrogen producing factories. No hydrogen, no balloon bombs. Taken together, these factors influenced ending the balloon campaign.

"Second question, how did the 555th get involved with the balloon bombs?"

"Getting right to the heart of the matter, aren't you?" Gramps interjected.

"About time," Garvey's dad added.

"Let's sleep on that one, guys. Will get to that topic in the morning. It's late, but still early enough for frozen pizza and some cards. What do you say? Poker anyone? A few cold beers... A few off-color jokes... Nice way to end the day."

"Sprague, are you trying to make money off us?" Gramps asked, smiling as he did so.

"As much as possible."

"I'm in," Garvey's dad said.

"What about you, Garvey? Ever play poker?"

"Watched. That's all."

"Well, it's time to improve your education. Okay with you guys?"

"Sure. Why not? Just don't mention anything to your mother," Garvey's dad admonished. "I'd like to live a little longer."

"And nothing to Grandma. She'll put arsenic in my soup if she finds out."

"What about a beer, Dad? I'm sixteen."

"Same deal. Discretion."

"Censorship?" Garvey asked.

"Survival."

The moon that rose over Moses Lake also shone over Seattle, where two women were sharing wine and female intuitiveness in the backyard of Garvey's home.

"Blair, you know what they're doing, don't you?"

"Probably eating frozen pizza."

"And playing poker," Grandma added.

"With beer."

"Probably initiating Garvey to a few tall ones."

"My poor baby," Blair moaned. "Trapped with those guys."

"And they'll tell dirty jokes. No doubt about that."

"And they will deny everything if we bring up the topic," Blair said with a knowing smile."

"Let's do it anyway. It's fun watching my old guy squirm."

"Another glass of wine, Grandma?"

"Why not? And a toast, to the 555th, thanks for this little respite."

CHAPTER 15

OPERATION FIRE FLY

<u>MOSES LAKE – THE NEXT DAY</u>

"Great breakfast. Mr. Sprague."

"Garvey, by the way you've finished off two helpings of eggs, bacon, hot buttered sourdough buns, there're either starving you at home, or you're a growing kid."

"Knocking the heck out of our food budget, I can tell you that," Garvey's father said in a manner suggesting he was resigned to his refrigerator being a 'glutton for punishment.'"

"He's not that bad, Matt," Gramps joined in. "Hell, if I remember correctly, you did considerable damage to the fridge, as did your football buddies, who played pool during their long lunch break in our house. Couldn't keep enough ham and cheese, pickles, mayo, and bread in the place."

"My dad cut school?" Garvey asked, a mischievous smile on his face. "And after all the lectures I've heard about that."

"It wasn't cutting. Lunch ran into football practice. I needed energy before butting heads."

"As did your buddies, one hell of an excuse," Gramps said jokingly.

Up early and ready to learn more about the 555th, the guys were in Sprague Junior's kitchen finishing off a great farm breakfast. Scattered through the night, they had slept soundly in separate rooms in the old farmhouse. That there was some serious snoring there can be no question. Tightly closed doors alleviated most of the atmospherics, permitting guests to sleep snug under layers of blankets and quilts. That is, except for Sprague's dog. He whimpered through the night, obviously distressed by the occasional and unfamiliar loud snorts. All that was forgotten, though, in the warmth of the kitchen and with stomachs full.

"Fellows, I'll get to the dishes later. Time to talk about the 555th. Before he died, my father did some research on the use of airborne troops in fighting forest fires here in Washington and throughout the west. I've kept my hand in it since, that is, both hands and two feet, one of my very few passions. If I say so myself, this is a topic I know well, one I'm delighted to share. Strangely, the story begins in California in early 1945.

"The Army and the U.S. Forestry Service had asked the State Division of Forestry to play a large role in protecting the West Coast from the balloon bombs and potential forest fires. But not just to protect valuable timber needed for the war effort. The Army was afraid fires might serve as beacons to an enemy fleet or submarines. As for the Navy, the admirals didn't want fog and smoke mixing. Made it too easy for the enemy to approach the coast. This was particularly true during the first two years of the war with Japan, even before the balloon bombs.

"The Division took on the job. All very hush. No loose tongues. Park rangers and isolated lookouts were alerted. Equipment was stored in the most vulnerable areas. Manpower, however, was at a premium. Most of the Division's trained personnel had been drafted into the services, leaving only the oldest guys around, and too few of them. The military's task was daunting. Men were needed. To fight fires. But where would they come from?

"There were, as it turned out, three possible groups the Division might utilize. The first was the armed forces. The Division prevailed upon the Army to establish three camps in Northern California made up of men who were about to be discharged. Instead of scattering these men in hometowns around the country, the idea was to place them in the camps until the threat was over. In this way, the Division's regular fire fighters would be augmented. And, after all, how much longer could Japan last? Iwo Jima was history. Okinawa lay ahead, but the war, terrible in its destruction, was coming to a bloody end. It was just a matter of time."

"This helped?" Gramps asked.

"Yes, but only on the ground."

"I don't understand," Garvey said. "Aren't fires on the ground?"

"Of course. But they're not always easily accessible. Good roads, whether built by the State, or punched in by the lumber companies, don't go everywhere. The Division needed men to drop in on a fire, so to speak."

"Parachutists!"

"Right on, Garvey. Smoke jumpers! The Division had a few, mainly older guys, not young enough for the war. The draft has depleted the Division's ranks. By 1944 the situation was desperate. It was worse in Washington more so than in any other state. There were only five smoke jumpers in the state. More were needed in case the balloon bombs, emulating lightning strikes, caused fires increasingly in remote areas. More 'jumpers' were needed along the coast. The combined Division need in California for men on the ground and others in the air, was met partially by an unexpected second source, conscientious objectors."

"C.O.'s," Gramps said, expelling the letters like they were bullets. "Guys who refused to fight."

"For religious reasons, I believe."

"We never talked about this, dad."

"People whose religious convictions precluded going to war? Yes, you're right. The topic never came up."

"Like the Mennonites, Anabaptists, and Quakers," Sprague added. "Killing was a mortal sin for them, jeopardizing their very souls. A C.O. claimed the right to refuse military service as a constitutional right of freedom of thought, conscience, or religion."

"In other words, they found a legal way out of the draft," Garvey's dad said with a sharpness to his voice.

"Easy, Matt," Gramps quickly replied. "One of the C.O.'s was a hero to you."

"Who?"

"Muhammad Ali."

"That's right, Matt," Sprague said. "He refused to go to Vietnam. What was his famous quote? 'I ain't got no quarrel with them Viet Cong. They never called me nigger.'

ALI – THE CHAMPION

Ali spoke his mind, as did a guy named Desmond T. Doss."

"Who" asked Garvey?"

"A C.O. who went to war."

"That doesn't make sense."

"It does, Garvey, if you choose to be medic. He served in the Pacific. Doss refused to kill. Enlisted only to save lives. He was one of only three C.O.'s who received the Medal of Honor for saving the lives of his comrades. Doss received his citation from President Truman in 1946.

TRUMAN AND DOSS

"How did they get out of the draft?" Garvey asked. "And how did they end up with the Division of Forestry?"

"That's a story that began in 1917."

"What?"

———————————

"The conscription law of that year gave President Woodrow Wilson the authority to assign CO draftees to any noncombatant military role during the war. Specifically, that meant that C.O.'s were imprisoned in military facilities such as Fort Lewis (Washington), Fort Leavenworth (Kansas) or Alcatraz Island (California). It was assumed the C.O.'s would change their minds rather than being imprisoned. The treatment for these men, numbering more than 2,000, was harsh. They got short rations, solitary confinement, and physical abuse. One case comes to mind... John T. Neufeld was a conscientious objector who was sentenced to 15 years of hard labor in the Disciplinary Barracks at Leavenworth, Kansas. He was paroled to do dairy work and released after serving five months of his sentence. Others were less fortunate. Two C.O. draftees in particular died from severe physical abuse. Apparently, no C.O. agreed to be drafted.

"The Roosevelt administration wanted to avoid another situation with C.O.'s as a second war loomed on the horizon. The Selective Training and Service Act was passed on September 14, 1940. It included the following provision. 'Any such person claiming such exemption from combatant training and service shall in lieu of such induction, be assigned to work of national importance under civilian direction.' Surprisingly, the Army was happy with this law. It wouldn't have to deal with thousands of uncooperative draftees, who might spread their views to others. In short, out of sight, out of mind.

"C.O.'s were placed in a camp program under the auspices of the Civilian Public Service (C.P.S.). Camps were set up around the country for nearly 12,000 draftees, who were willing to serve their country short of military action with a rifle. The camps had plenty of important work to do: soil conservation, forestry, fire fighting, and agriculture. In some ways, the C.P.S. was like a remake of the old C.C.C. (Civilian Conservation Corps), which put young men to work during the Great Depression. Some of these men in the C.P.S. were even trained as smoke jumpers and were available when the balloon barrage began. They were quickly scoped up by the military and placed under civilian control within the U.S. Forestry Service. Even with this contingent, however, more men were needed."

———————

"The last resource was the Army," Sprague said. "However, paratroopers already stationed in Europe or the Pacific were unavailable to be smoke jumpers. Only one group of trained paratroopers was unassigned to a combat role."

"The 555th," Garvey said triumphantly."

"You read my thoughts."

———————

"After D-Day, the 555th figured they weren't going to Europe. Again, the major reason for this was segregation. European commanders from Eisenhower down, 'simply had no use' for Negro lack paratroopers. That was the raw truth. That fellow you researched, Garvey, Walter Morris, he was quoted on this matter: 'The Army had no place for us. None of the commanding generals wanted the extra problem of integrating colored soldiers with white soldiers, so they refused.'

"The Asian Theater of the war was different. The 555th still hoped to get into the war against the Japanese. But once more, bigotry and prejudice ended that hope in a most cruel manner. The word came down the 555th was being assigned to a war zone. Naturally, the officers and men thought they were headed to the Pacific to give General Douglas McArthur a hand. Then orders came through. Travel westward to Oregon. This led the 555th to believe that it would disembark from Portland or Seattle for the Pacific conflict. But as Morris recounted, 'It wasn't until we arrived in Oregon that we learned we'd be fighting the Japanese on the fire line in the Western United States.'

"The California Division of Forestry and the U.S. Forestry Service had tapped the last resource. The 555th was the only trained paratrooper group available to become smoke jumpers. The decision was made in the White House. Colored soldiers would be used to confront the Japanese balloon bomb attacks. They soldiers would be part of a highly secret operation code-named Fire-Fly. Over the next year, the 555th would make over 1200 individual jumps to 36 fires, a record that still stands today. All of this was done out of the limelight and was almost totally unknown to the general public. In no way was the work of the 555th celebrated in the white press. Nor did the Negro press of the time, because of censorship, pick up on the story. The government, fearing public hysteria, concealed information about the balloon bombs as well as the colored soldiers who fought them.

"The 555th was actually sent to two camps, Pendleton, Oregon, and Chico, California. There their mission was explained. They would be on emergency call to rush 'to forest fires in any of several western states and to join with the forest service men in suppressing the blaze.' However, another mission, equally important, awaited the 555th. It would be 'prepared to move into areas where there were suspected Japanese bombs, cordon off the area, locate the bombs, and dispose of them.'"

"Wait a darn minute," Gramps said. "Those guys weren't trained for that kind of stuff, either fighting fires or dealing with Jap bombs."

"Not at first. But they did get it," Sprague replied. "Oh, did they get it!"

———————————————

"The men of the 555th knew how to jump from airplanes. They had been taught how to land on flat land. Now they had to learn how to land on forested mountainsides, a whole different bag of beans, more difficult and dangerous than anything they had encountered before. They knew how to handle parachute lines, but they had never used a new type of parachute with shroud lines, 'which permitted circling maneuvers,' hopefully to keep the smoke jumper from landing in a 200-foot high trees, bristling rocks, or a creek plunging headlong down a gorge. This is where Frank Derry comes in."

"Who?"

"The savior of the 555th, Garvey. He had invented the 'Derry-chute.' By pulling a white shroud line, men could turn themselves in a 360-degree circling movement. This gave them a wider choice of landing areas. But it took lots of training to do this."

"And Derry provided the training?"

"Absolutely, Garvey. Derry was the right man for the training. He had been involved in the first recorded 'smoker jumper' experiment on July 12, 1940. As the pilot, he was at the controls of a propeller-driven plane in the skies above a lightning-triggered fire in Idaho's Nez Perce Forest. Two men were in the plane with him, Rufus Robinson and Earl Cooley. They were going to make the first known smoke jump. Their training had been, to say the least, rudimentary.

EARL COOLEY, SMOKEJUMPER

A parachute was hung from a tree. The harness, shroud lines and release handles were pointed out to the two men. That was it. Cooley later admitted, 'We didn't know what we were doing.' Robinson was first out of the plane and made it down without incident. Cooley, on the other hand, had twisted lines and was almost in free fall before the lines cleared. He landed without injury after clipping the limbs off a big spruce tree. Then, as he said, came the hard part. After putting out the fire, 'we had to walk 28-miles to the nearest ranger station.'"

"The 555th underwent additional training. The men had been taught how to fight an entrenched foe. Now they learned the techniques of fighting a forest fire and how to use forestry equipment for that purpose. This was done over a three-week period. They also learned how to survive in wooded areas --- how to deal with broken bones and other injuries. They learned how to descend from a tree, using rope techniques. And they had demolition training."

"New skills for the job."

"And new equipment, Garvey. Instead of a steel military helmet, they were given football helmets with wire mesh face protectors. The mesh screen was important. It protected the face from a number of things, tree branches, hot embers, insects, and rocks. While they still wore their standard army fatigues, air corps fleece-lined flying jacket and trousers were worn over the old stuff. Heavy gloves were standard equipment, but they were not worn during a jump. Bare hands, no matter how cold it was, were needed to manipulate the parachute."

"What about wilderness training?" Garvey's dad asked. "For the most part, these were guys from cities."

"Right on, Matt. Perhaps the most difficult training was the physical demands on the men of the 555th. Most had never climbed in heavily forested areas, or mountainous terrain, or up ravines, or across cascading streams, and at night no less. They now learned how to do this with the help of forest rangers. The rangers 'could walk up the hills like a cat on a snake walk' was the way one soldier described them. The rangers were 'a fine group of men,' who adequately prepared the colored soldiers for what was ahead of them. They taught the men how to climb and how to use an axe. What vegetation to eat. And how to read forest service maps."

"And they did it without bias?" Garvey asked.

"They were fair-minded men and they understood the risks involved. They were professionals. The soldiers would be prepared. And they were. By mid-July, the entire 555th battalion had qualified as 'smoke jumpers.' This was the Army's first and only airborne fire-fighters unit. It was an honor deserved by the men and almost totally unknown by the outside world."

SUITED UP

LEAPING INTO THE SKY

———————

"Doesn't seem fair," Garvey said with youthful idealism. "All that training, all the jumps they made, and no public acclaim."

"No question about that," Sprague quickly responded. Still, smoke jumping was something. Walter Morris summed up the situation, stating:"

We were trained, but we had nowhere to go. That was when the Agriculture Department (U.S. Forestry Service) asked the Army if they could spare a few paratroopers to train them as smoke jumpers to combat the Japanese incendiary balloons that were flown over the jet stream from Japan to the Pacific coast line. So the Army told the Agriculture Department they could have the whole battalion.

"Morris also touched on a related topic. Given the prejudice and segregation, not only in the general society, but also in the Army, why would any colored soldier want to fight anyone, or take on a forest fire? Why would any guy want to risk his life? His answer was right on point:

This was my country; this is my duty regardless of the social climate; regardless of the faults. This is my country, my children's country and their children's. It is up to me and many people of all races and cultures to fight the haters and racists to make this a better place to live.

"Another member of the Triple Nickels, Charles Stevens, who had enlisted in the Army to prove a better life for his wife and new baby, put it this way. When "I joined the 555th, I finally felt like I belonged to something.'"

———————————

"That's the story," Sprague said.

"Not completely," Gramps quickly retorted. "There's still another chapter."

"You know something, don't you?" Garvey's dad asked.

"Unhappily, I do."

"What?" Garvey questioned.

"Jumping Jim Crow was alive and well in Oregon."

"You know about Oregon?" Sprague said, more a statement than a question.

Gramps didn't reply. He just looked at his son, Matt, and then glanced at Garvey before speaking. It was as if he needed them in particular to hear what he had to say.

———————————

"Pendleton Air Base was in Umatilla County, in northeastern Oregon. It was located outside the town of Pendleton on a plateau overlooking the good Oregon folks. B-29 crews had trained there. All white crews. The based had been "skeletonized" once the B-29 bomber crews were gone. That is, after the 'bomb.' It was on a "caretaker status." The place was barren. Hardly anyone was there except for the 555th, control tower personnel and a small engineer maintenance group. All the men ate together. There was no real problem among them. A full colonel, however, commanded the base. He quickly made it known to the 555th that 'he disliked having an all-Black unit at his station.' But he was stuck with a reinforced company of 160 colored soldiers and eight officers. He made it difficult for colored and white officers to mix beyond the mess hall. Inspections of the colored barracks were done with 'undue meticulousness.'. Given this, he was just another prejudiced officer the 555th had to contend with, as they had in Georgia and North Carolina. But surprisingly, as bad as it was in the South, things were worse in Pendleton.

"The people in town weren't used to seeing Black soldiers. Regrettably, many shared the same sentiments as the base commander. It was difficult to buy a drink in town or to get a meal. Only two bars in a town of 12,000 would serve drinks and only one restaurant would serve Negroes. Accommodations for family members were almost non-existent. Prejudice was not limited to the 555[5th.] Tensions with minorities had a long history in Oregon. In the nineteenth century, it was with the Chinese, bigotry, discrimination, and violence. In the first part of the twentieth century the Japanese became the targets. In the 1920's, the Ku Klux Klan had a strong resurgence in Oregon with a vehement distaste for Catholics, foreigners, and Negroes. It wasn't exactly the overt Jim Crowism of the Deep South, but it was bad enough. And all this occurred while the 555th was trying to protect the good citizens of Pendleton and save their forests from destruction. Of course, no one ever said racial bias was rationale."

––––––––––––––

"The people of Pendleton were stupid," Garvey bellowed. "Idiots."

"Many of them had migrated from the South," Sprague said. "The Oregon Trail wasn't made up of saints, only people looking for open land. They brought with them their hopes and dreams, and their biases.

That's just the way it was. Oregon was a territory. All were invited. No border guard checked your prejudices."

"Just like today," Garvey said. "People still move around with their ugly views, right dad?"

"I wish it were otherwise."

"Remember, then as now," Gramps said, "not everyone was prejudiced. Lots of people befriended the 555th, especially after the incident. Everyone always expected injuries. Jumping from a C-47 was dangerous. Landing on unforgiving terrain was dangerous. Scaling down ponderosas was dangerous. Facing a blazing forest fire was dangerous. And if you leap into space 120 individual times, things will happen. More than thirty members of the 555th suffered injuries, ranging from "cuts and bruises to broken legs and crushed chests." Some experienced asphyxiation. Yes, injuries were expected, but no one anticipated a fatality."

"A smoke jumper died, Gramps?"

"Yes."

CHAPTER 16

A DEATH IN THE TREES

Gramps continued:

"The incident and the man… Not much is known about Malvin L. Brown; his military records are sketchy. No military photographs are available. He was the only 555th fatality.

"This is what is known. He was twenty-two-years old on October 11, 1942. On that day, he took a fateful step. He walked into a Philadelphia Army recruiting station and signed up. He was a nice kid with a limited grammar school education, a job driving trucks, and a wife. He completed basic training. That's when he heard about an all-volunteer Negro paratrooper unit. Along with many other Blacks, he tried to transfer into the new unit. Another fateful step had been taken. He met the requirements for entry and was accepted into the newly formed 555th Parachute Infantry Battalion.

BROWN AND HIS SON

"He took his paratrooper training at Fort Benning, as well as classes to be a medic. When orders were issued for the 555th to report to a new permanent duty station in Pendleton, Oregon, Brown went along. On Monday, August 6, 1945, an emergency call came in for military smoke jumpers. A large fire had erupted near Lemon Butter, 38-miles northeast of Roseburg in the Umpqua National Forest. The fire was burning in tall timber where 200-foot tall trees were very common.

"No one is quite sure what happened. What went wrong…? The winds were heavy. Gusts were chaotic. Nerves were on edge. The adrenaline was flowing. Each jumper, though skilled and confident, struggled to control his fear. Going out the door of the C-47 frightened every man in that type of weather.

"The pilot had made the decision for a one thousand foot drop, about two-hundred-feet below the standard drop altitude. This was not going to be an easy jump. Many of the smoke jumpers anticipated having trouble controlling their chutes, avoiding obstacles, and landing in the drop zone. And they were right.

"Apparently, Brown landed in a tall fir tree, 200 feet above the ground. He attempted to slide down his rope after landing. He only had 50-feet of rope for what was called a 'let-down.' It's conjectured that he somehow lost his hold on the rope. He fell over 150-feet into a rocky creek bed at the base of the tree. The later medical report indicated death was instantaneous. The cause of death was officially listed as 'basal skull fracture' and 'cerebral hemorrhage.'

"After dealing with the fire, Brown's body was carried out the next day by his buddies to the nearest town some 15-miles away. They weren't about to leave him. He was their friend. It was their obligation to take him home. Once this was done, his remains were placed on a train. Four days later he arrived in Narberh, Pennsylvania. There his body was turned over to his wife, Edna, whom he had married just before entering the Army. Shortly thereafter, he was buried. The exact location of his burial site is unknown to this day.

"Brown was twenty-four years old when he died. But he was not forgotten. In recognition of the 555th's work in battling the Lemon Butte Fire, the Umpqua National Forest named an overlook 'Fireman's Leap.' It was from this overlook that forest employees had watched the 555th jump. The 555th would not be forgotten. By remembering Brown, they also remembered all the Black soldiers who leaped into the sky above Oregon.

"The official dedication for Brown read:

On August 6, 1945 PFC Malvin L. Brown, a member of the 555th Parachute Infantry Battalion, died in the line of duty while on initial attack of a wildfire by the name of Lemon Butte on the Umpaqua National Forest.

"Continuing, the dedication said:

He (Brown) and 200 or so paratroopers had been trained to be Smokejumpers at Pendleton, Oregon. They had been called in because during 1944, Japan had begun sending balloons to North America, via the jet stream, which carried five firebombs and a standard explosive. Their plan was to start multiple wildfires and drawn fighting troops away from the war effort. This threat was real and on-way the U.S. hoped to defend against this threat was to cross train paratroopers as smoke jumpers.

"The dedication concluded as follows:"

Malvin landed in the top of a fir tree that was 180 to 200 feet tall. As he tried to get to the ground on the 50-foot let-down rope he had been given he somehow lost his hold on the rope and fell into some rocks at the base of the tree and died.

———————————

"That's quite a story, Gramps."

"Isn't it, Garvey? But not the whole story."

"What are you getting at?"

"What was missing in the dedication?"

"Missing?"

"A key point."

Garvey looked at the others. Blank faces stared back at him. No help there. What key point, he thought? He thought about what Gramps had said. His recitation of the dedication, almost word by words. Then it hit him. The most obvious thing; the key to the 555th and to everything that was their story was absent. He smiled a sad smile.

"Got it, have you?" Gramps asked.

"The dedication didn't mention that Brown was Black. It didn't mention that the 555th battalion was an all-Black unit."

"Meaning?"

"Unless you knew that…"

"Yes?"

"You would assume Brown was white, as was the 555th."

"And?"

"You would be forgotten, written out of history."

"Exactly."

"Purposefully?"

"Intentionally? I don't think so, Garvey. Perhaps just an oversight; I'm afraid we'll never know. There is so little by which to remember him."

The three men were quiet. What was there to say? Eventually, the silence was broken.

"So what now?" Garvey asked.
"We go home." Garvey's Dad said.
"The story is done?" Sprague questioned.
"Almost." Gramps stated matter-of-factly. "Almost."
"Dad, what's Gramps up to?"
"I'm not sure. Sprague?"
"He hasn't said a thing to me."
"Gramps?"
"Kansas."

BRAVE MEN NOT TO BE FORGOTTEN

CHAPTER 17

LETTING GO

<u>THREE WEEKS LATER - SEATTLE</u>

"Matt, I'm sorry. I can't give my consent."
"The airline tickets are already bought, Blair."
"Gramps can return them."
"Garvey will be disappointed."
"He'll deal with it."
"We need to keep talking."
"We've been talking for two hours."
"Than we'll continue until…"
"… I change my mind?"

Garvey's parents were in their kitchen, which was a battleground of sort. They were testing the outer limits of marital bliss. Their son was the focus of their conversation. Lines had been drawn. Blair didn't want her son going to Kansas. Matt was more amiable to the idea. A betting man wouldn't have given even odds as to who would win this argument.

"He's going to miss school again."
"Honey, we've been through this already. Garvey's teachers are okay with it. Just two days, that's all. They leave Thursday night and return in the later afternoon on Monday. Just a weekend to complete the final research."

"Did you fix it with the teachers, Matt? Tell me the truth."
"No."
"Garvey?"
"With help."
"Who?"
"Gramps."

To say that Blair bristled at that would be an understatement... Here we go again, she thought. That "old" man is butting into our family life. He's turning my son into a vagabond. First Moses Lake, now Kansas. Whatever happened to just using the library or the Internet? Why this intense need to fly halfway across the country? And jeopardizing our son's grades again. Who does he think he is anyway?

"We're Garvey's parents. Gramps shouldn't speak for us at the school. That's our job."
"It is."
"So?"
"He was pretty convincing."
"You knew about this?"
"After the fact."
"I bet."

Matt chose to ignore Blair's comment. She was upset. No question about that and maybe with good reason. Gramps should have talked to us first. Springing the surprise as a done deal wasn't a very good idea. His dad, he reflected, needed to stop this stuff. He needed to lighten up about the 555th. He and Garvey could go to Kansas during the Spring Break. Why did it have to be now? Why was it necessary to cause a family ruckus?

"What did he work out at school, Matt?"
"He went to all of Garvey's teachers."
"During class?"
"On their breaks."
"And?"

"He showed them Garvey's research to date."

"And?"

"They were really impressed, especially the English teacher, Mrs. Cornelius, and his A.P. History teacher. No problem with either of them. In fact, they encouraged him to go?"

"What?"

"They're in on this. Garvey will get double credit for the final research paper. And he has to make a presentation before each class. Even the principal got involved?"

"Gramps saw him?"

"Talked about a multicultural day to honor "all Americans who fought in our wars.""

"The principal bought it?"

"Gramps was persuasive. One thing, though."

"There's always one thing with Gramps."

"Not with Gramps, but with the principal. Garvey must, as a member of the Student Council Class, organize the day. Lots of work involved."

"You're a Superintendent… You buy this? And what about his other teachers?"

"Different school district. And I'm not an administrator in this one. I'm his father. And the other teachers are cool."

"Meaning."

"Garvey wants to go. Virgin Kansas Airlines to Kansas City nonstop, a rather short hop. Three and half hours, then thirty miles up the road in a rental car to Fort Leavenworth."

"You want him to go, don't you?"

"As do you, heart of heart."

"You think so?"

"I know you."

Matt had struck pay dirt. Blair really didn't want to stand in Garvey's way. Nor was she particularly angry at Gramps. It was something else she had to reluctantly admit, though it was difficult. Her son was growing older. He was growing up and away from her and Matt. Was this what was troubling her? She knew he was no longer her little boy. Physically, he was a man. Emotionally, he wasn't far behind. Intellectually, he was gifted. And she was happy with all this. She just didn't want to lose him. Not yet anyway. When it was time for college, okay. Or the beautiful young thing he'd bring home one day, okay. But Fort Leavenworth? My God, that place was a former federal prison! It was a lonely outpost on the frontier for years.

"He's just doing what we did, Blair. Testing the waters. I guess it's called growing up. It had to happen."

"I know."

"Hell, they'll have a good time."

"But why Fort Leavenworth?"

"Gramps said, 'they're expected,' whatever that means."

"Who is expecting them?"

"I told you. I don't know."

"You're really okay with this?"

"Yes, Blair. Yes, I really am."

"You're not putting me on?"

"No."

"Then I better start packing his suitcase."

CHAPTER 18

NOTES

The Virgin Kansas plane was a late model Boeing X331, two-engine commute plane with old-fashioned service, especially lunch with on-the-house drinks. Of course, you had to sit in the premium seats for that, shelling out lots of cash for that privilege, which Gramps had done without hesitation. As he rationalized it, "Hell, I'm ninety years old. Time to start enjoying myself. First class is first class."

Now high above Montana, he glanced over at his grandson, who was asleep, dead to the world. "Great kid," he thought. But tired. His teachers had worked him hard before the trip, extra assignments, more severe grading or so it seemed. Garvey hadn't flinched. With a smile he did what was asked. His parents didn't even have to push. But all that work had kept him from working on the 555th. Before drifting into his nocturnal peace, Garvey had asked him to look over some disjointed notes and some photographs. And that's what Gramps was doing, if he could just figure out how to make the Garvey's Apple tablet work.

––––––––––––––

Quotes by the War Department 1950

#1 - "Although Black Americans had a legacy of demonstrated bravery in combat throughout history, white Americans had relegated Blacks to performing menial tasks in service units to perpetuate stereotypical beliefs."

CIVIL WAR SOLDIERS

#2 – The 555th Parachute Infantry Battalion challenged these limitations and became one of the first elite all-Black units in the Army. With the Army leaders and the War Department observing, they became a catalyst for changing how Blacks would be utilized in the Army. They were the new Buffalo Soldiers.

THE BUFFALO SOLDIERS ON THE FRONTIER

Pentagon Quote - 1996

"They (the 555th} kicked open the door. They took the door off the hinges. Others had done it during the Spanish-America War."

THE SPANISH-AMERICAN WAR, 1898

Bradley Biggs – Member of the 555th 1981

"They (the 555th) shunted the windows of the past (segregation) and dominated this scene by values of character, drive, pride, and unit."

BLACK SOLDIERS IN WORLD WAR I

U.S. Forestry Service – 1975

"The Triple Nickels became not only the first military fire fighting force unit in the world, but pioneered methods of combating forest fires that are still used today."

THE TRIPLE NICKELS

Japanese Internment Organization – 1983

"The conduct of the Triple Nickels contributed immensely to the well-being of most Japanese-Americans in internment camps. If it were known that the Japanese balloons had been successful in reaching our shores, there is no telling what additional maltreatment would have befallen the internees."

INTERNMENT CAMP

U.S. Department of Agriculture – 1990 – Tom Tidwell, Department Chief

"These highly skilled paratroopers used their military training in a different kind of combat few people were aware of. Fighting the fires that had the potential to do great harm to the nation in a time of war was dangerous, important work. We are extremely pleased to honor them at our national headquarters for their heroic service to the Agency and the nation making more than 1,200 individual jumps during the summer of 1945."

ANOTHER JUMP

Garvey's Notes – Tidwell might have added it was hard, smoky, dirty sweaty, dangerous work. It took courage and audacity to jump from a C-47 into a fire below, cut off from civilization and depending on each other for everything --- food, water, and first aid.

PREPARING FOR ANOTHER DIRTY JOB

National 555th Museum – 1995 – Paul Galloway, Executive Director

"It (the museum) highlights a piece of history that a lot of people just don't realize. The African-American Soldiers served when segregation was still going on. These guys had to be the best of the best. They served during a time when the Army trusted them to jump out of airplanes, but did not trust them to fight. It was during a time when it was not safe to get off the buses for fear of death when they traveled to Army bases in the South. We think it's important that Soldiers know their history. They need to know where they came from so they can be inspired to be the best Soldiers they can be."

Gramps looked up from Garvey's notes. He closed the computer. He needed to rest. He needed a drink. Something strong. Hell with the doctors. He ordered a gin and tonic, suggesting to the flight attendant the she go heavy on the gin and light on the tonic. Something was on his mind. The drink might help.

What had he just read, he asked himself? Something about "soldiers need to know where they came from." That was it; one should know "where he came from." He pondered the phrase. Was that why he was on this trip to Kansas with Garvey? Was that why they had been to Moses Lake? All the research, all the checking through old records, it all had mean something. Was it all about knowing where you came from? But who needed to know? Surely not an old man with nine decades in the books, or did he? He knew where he was from. He knew where he had been. Could it be Garvey? But if so, why? What was it he needed to know? What was it I wanted him to know?

Gramps turned back to Garvey's notes. Too darn many questions, he thought. Time to get to them later.

Garvey's Notes About General James M. Gavin – 1946

This was the "jumping general," who earned his reputation by jumping with his men during combat in WWII. This was also the "color-blind general," who ordered the integration of the 555th into the 82nd Airborne, December 1947, almost seven months before President Harry S. Truman signed Executive Order 998. That act established "equality of treatment and opportunity in the Armed Forces for people of all races, religions, and national origins."

JAMES M. GAVIN

<u>General Gavin – 1947</u>

"It was time for change. Segregation was a serious problem, and one not to be taken lightly, for our Army had been a two-colored army for a long time."

<u>Walter Morris – 1946</u>

"I think we were crying for two different reasons. We were glad that segregation was leaving the Army and we were sorry we were losing the Triple Nickel colors."

<u>John Rucker - 1950 – Member of the 555th</u>

It took more than five years to fully integrate the Armed Forces. Rucker remembered how difficult it was to overcome resistance in the services. "Back in the old days, when your orders were cut, they had your name, and if you were Black, the words, 'negro enlisted,' came after your name. After we integrated, they stopped putting those words on orders, but instead used a code to describe who you were – 'one' for white and 'two' for black. The first sergeant at each company would have a roster of everybody with the codes. They weren't supposed to know our color, but they knew. And during basic training at Fort Knox, although every Soldier sat in the same classroom, but at the end of the day, the white soldiers went to one barracks and the Black solders went to separate barracks."

<u>Garvey's Notes - Walter Morris – March 10, 2010</u>

The Pentagon honored the 555th. At the age of 89, Walter Morris attended the ceremony. It was said of him that he "helped convince the Army that Black soldiers had the courage and intellect to become paratroopers." After the ceremony, Morris said, "I feel like if I could only enlist again and be with all these wonderful people again it would be the greatest thing in my life."

Garvey's Notes - General Gavin's Fair-minded Decision

The New York City Victory Parade was held in January 1946. General Gavin decided to include the 555th in the parade up Fifth Avenue. He didn't have to do this. The 555th had not fought in Europe. In had not been in combat anywhere. But he knew what the Black soldiers had done in Project Fire-Fly. He permitted them to march and wear the symbols of the 82nd's proud record. "His vision and respect for the Black soldier was very much different from that of his contemporaries."

INCLUDED AT LAST

————————————

"Wake up Gramps. We're about to land."
"I guess I drifted off."
"My notes must have put you to sleep."
"Not likely."
"I didn't really tie them together yet in any real fashion."
"They spoke for themselves, Garvey."

CHAPTER 19

VOICES

The drive to Fort Leavenworth was uneventful. After renting a car at the Kansas City airport, Gramps and Garvey took Interstate 70 westward, then turned north on State 7. Gramps drove slowly and carefully as befitting his age. In time they were at the Fort, which was on the west side of the Missouri River, the great waterway Lewis and Clark navigated upstream in 1804. Military personnel checked them into the Fort. They were here to visit the 555th Parachute Infantry Company Monument. Directions to the monument site were given. A few minutes later, Gramps stopped the rental on the side of the road not far from the monument. Quietly, they exited the car about 30-yards from the monument.

"We're here to see a monument, Gramps?"
"That's part of it."
"And?"
"I'm not too sure."
"You're being evasive."
"Not this time."

For reasons he couldn't fathom Garvey was a bit taken aback by Gramps' response. "Not this time…" There was a degree of candidness to the words, suggesting an unusual clarity not yet understood by the young man. Something was different. Where Gramps was usually one step ahead of the crowd this did not seem true, at least at this moment.

As they walked toward the monument they passed others, many tourists, some of course, were family in some way with the hard stone. Though little was said as they walked there was a quiet acknowledgement in the air that this was a special place honoring special men.

Up closer, they could see the bust of a paratrooper on top of a hexagonal granite base. The bronze bust faced away from the Missouri River.

They approached the monument. Both Gramps and Garvey had the strangest feeling the helmeted face was looking at them, as if to welcome them. As if it had been waiting.

"Gramps, the face is familiar."
"It is."
"I've seen photographs of this man."
"Go on."
"It's 1st Sgt. Walter Morris."
"Yes."
"You knew about this monument before we started?"
"I did, Garvey."
"Why are we here then?"
"Wrong question. Why did I bring you here?"
"Okay. Why?"
"To find yourself, young man."
"Gramps, I don't understand."
"Look at the bust. What do you see?"

SGT. WALTER MORRIS

"An African-American. A Black soldier."

"Noting else?"

"Jumping Jim Crow has been vanquished."

"Meaning?"

"A Black soldier could stand with pride. He was as good as anyone else."

"And anything else?"

"His chute is packed, probably perfectly, as if he was getting ready for inspection."

"He's a Black paratrooper, Garvey!"

"I know that."

"Going back into the generations of his family, there's been the mixing of black and white blood."

"Probably."

"As with you, Garvey?"

Garvey stared at Gramps. What was he saying? Garvey knew his father was white. He knew his mother was Black. And he knew his other grandfather, Gartha, was Black, and that Teresa, his wife, was white. Old news... So what! He knew kids from lots of mixed families. It wasn't a big deal. Some people even said it was the new normal.

"Remember the Galloway quote? 'We need to remember where we've come from?'"

"Sure."

"Well, you share a history with Sgt. Morris. He helped to make the country better for Blacks. For you, Garvey."

"I wasn't even alive during the war."

"He fought for the future. For the unborn, for you."

"You make it sound so personal, Gramps."

"For him and others in the 555th, it was. The monument reminds us of the sacrifices his generation made. It asks us to not forget what they did. It's reaching out to you, Garvey. Just look at the bust. Look at the sorrow mixed in with hope. Look at the determination to make things better. He wanted to achieve equality and dignity as a Black man in our society. He wanted to have opportunities. It's all there in his face. Look closely and you'll see yourself and generations of other young men."

Garvey was unsure what to make of all this. Once more, he stared at the bust, which now seemed pliable, almost animated, as if it wanted to speak to him.

And then it happened.

He heard the words, or, as he recalled later, thought he did.

"Garvey, I'm glad your grandfather brought you here. It's good to see you and all the other young men brought here by their families. I can't shake your hand, but you know I'd liked to. I can see that you're a fine young person, tall and strong, sensitive and smart, and I'm sure a good student. You have made a fine member of the 555th. We'd have been proud to call you a paratrooper. I'm glad we kicked in those doors so you could have a better life. Keep kicking them in for yourself and others. And don't

forget us, as we tried never to forget you. And take care of Gramps. He's come a long way to make this visit."

Garvey glanced around. No one else, it appeared, had heard the words. What was going on? Was his mind playing tricks on him?

"Garvey, you okay?"
"Gramps…"
"What is it?"
"Did you hear?"
"Hear what?"

What could Garvey say? It was like that old movie he once watched with his dad, the one with Kevin Costner playing Ray Kinsella, who hears strange voices in his cornfield. *Field of Dreams*, that's what the movie was called. No one believed Ray at first. Old-time baseball players just don't talk to transplanted city guys amongst the cornstalks of Iowa. Or did they? It was probably better, Garvey reasoned to just keep mum. He had heard something, though --- *"And don't forget us, as we tried never to forget you."* Those words kept ringing in his mind.

"Earth to Garvey. Come in. What did you hear?"
"Nothing, Gramps. Let's check the granite panels."
"You sure?"
"Sure."

On three sides of the monument were inscribed panels. The first panel was entitled **"THE ORIGINAL SEVENTEEN"** Listed were the names of the first volunteers selected for the 555th. The list was headed by1st Sgt. Walter Morris… All of them but one had qualified as paratroopers on February 8, 1944. The seventeenth soldier had been ill. He qualified the next week. Names engraved in stone… But Garvey knew that behind each name was a face, a young Black who put his life on the line so long ago. Looking at the names, he felt an immense pride in what they had done.

The second panel was **"DEDICATED TO THE FIRST BLACK PARACHUTE INFANTRY."** It listed significant dates in the history of the 555th.

. *Authorized as the 555*[th] *– December 19, 1943*
. *Activated as the 555*[th] *– November 25, 1944*
. *Inactivated – December 15, 1947*

The panel also quoted Lt. General David H. Petraeus, the famous leader of American troops in the second Iraqi War: "These great paratroopers walked point for their race and for our country facing down discrimination by 'standing in the door' as one and jumping into our nation's history."

The doorway, the open door of a C-47, that's what the General was talking about Garvey thought. The men were hooking up and checking their parachutes. The red light... The final word... "Go." Men leaping into the sky Garvey could see it all. He could feel the first moments of free fall, then the rough pull of the parachute opening, and finally the slow descent toward the forested canopy below. He could feel the cool air rushing by and the thump-thump of his heart. And then he was on the ground, collecting his chute, and yelling, "I made it."

The third panel mentioned dates and events --- *TRIPLE NICKLE AND SMOKE JUMPERS.* It also listed the first training jump (September 10, 1944) and the first death (Malvin L. Brown). It listed the names of the first Black officers assigned and qualified. Finally, it mentioned the *Fire-Fly Project* (the Secret Mission) and related significant dates and information (see previous page).

. *First Fire Jump – July 14, 1945*
. *Last Fire Jump – October 10, 1945.*
. *Total Fires Fought – 36*
. *Total Individual Jumps – 1200*

The monument was a sort of research paper in granite. Certainly, a summary of the 555th's history of thee brave men. As others viewed the monument, Garvey felt a pang in his chest, something between joy and sadness if that was possible. Clearly, he was delighted others had come to honor the 555th. At the same time, he was sad, for the visitors only knew what the monument stated, not all that he knew --- Jumping Jim Crow, the Black Codes, the Plessy Case, the "backroom deal," the "balloon bombs," and "Operation Fire-Fly. He made a silent promise at that moment to remedy that situation. Someday he would tell the whole story in a book. The past would no longer be vanquished.

Garvey turned to Gramps, saying, "Time to leave?"
"Not quite yet."
"Why?"
"Across the road... Look."

At first Garvey couldn't make sense out of what he was supposed to see. He saw the problem was the late afternoon sun already dipping in the west, yet shining brightly in his eyes.

"To your right, Garvey," Gramps called out. "At about 2:30."

Garvey shifted his stance and peered with greater concentration across the street. It was then that he saw it, a wall-like structure, not high but certainly long. On its face were three words: **_BUFFALO SOLDIER MONUMENT._**

"I see it, Gramps. Another stop?"
"I think we're expected."
"I don't understand."
"I'm a bit confused myself."
"Gramps."
"Not kidding, Garvey."
Gramps confused? Garvey wasn't sure. There it was again, some elusive mystery even to Gramps. Now this... Was it another of his deceptions? More manipulation? Or were his 90-years really catching up to him?

As they crossed the street and walked toward the monument, Garvey tried to figure out what Gramps was talking about. Immediately, they saw the famous Buffalo Soldier sculptured by Eddie Dixon. The Black soldier, pulling tightly on the reins of his rearing horse with one hand, a rifle held in the other. Though locked in place by bronze and granite, the man and horse seemed alive with action, as if they had come upon trouble and needed to act. The statue suggested strength and commitment, powerful qualities of the Buffalo Soldiers.

BUFFALO SOLDIER

"That's what I call a monument," Gramps said. "You just want to grab your rifle, saddle a horse, and ride off with that guy."

"Well, don't forget to take along your Medicare Card. It could be a long ride."

"You might be surprised what these old bones can still do."

"What's that?" Garvey asked, ignoring his grandfather's response.

"That's a special monument in this Memorial Park. Only one way you can get your name on the chunk of granite."

"Being wounded? Killed?"

"Sometimes."

Garvey walked up to the triangle-shaped monument. Again, he saw three large words chiseled into the rock --- **MEDALS OF HONOR.** He counted the names. Eight in all… He wondered about each man. What had he done to earn the country's highest medal for action "above and beyond the call of duty?" What great risk had each taken in the midst of battle? How many lives had been saved by their actions? And he wondered if he could be that brave?

"Gramps, when was this monument established?"

"July 25, 1992."

"By the President?"

"By Congress. It monument was officially opened by General Colin L. Powell. He was the chairman of the Joint Chiefs of Staff. As you may know, he was the first Black to serve in that capacity. He said a few appropriate words at the time."

"I've heard of him."

"He pointed out that it was in 1866 that the U.S. Congress authorized the formation of several Black regiments. One of these, the 10th Cavalry Regiment, was formed at Fort Leavenworth under the command of Col. Benjamin H. Grieson. We know that regiment today as the Buffalo Soldiers." He finished his brief remarks, saying:

The powerful purpose of this monument is to motivate us. To motivate us to keep struggling until all Americans have an equal seat at our national table, until all Americans enjoy every opportunity to excel, every chance to achieve their dream.

"He could have been talking about the 555th, Gramps."

"Perhaps he was."

"Same deal."

"What are you getting at, Garvey?"

"It's always the same struggle, equality and to be treated like a man."

Gramps merely smiled at Garvey's comment before saying, "Let's check out the last statute in the Memorial Park."

"Over there, Gramps," Garvey said, pointing out a large bust sitting atop of granite pillar with words carved on three sides. "

"I see it."

The bust had the face of a young Black wearing a Civil War period cap, looking outward with his arms folded together. Once more Garvey concentrated on the face, at the deep-set eyes and then at the hands toughened by hard work and the demands of war. He glanced back at the facial expression and thought barely out loud, "You seem at ease, whomever you are. There is no fear. You're past that. But there is no joy either. Just the feeling that you've seen too much of this world, stark and harsh, yet offering hope and opportunities. Who were you, he wondered? Or were you a contemporary model drawn from a hundred possibilities? Or are you a face from an old Civil War photograph, wrinkled and fading?

WHO WERE YOU?

Garvey peered hard and long at the face. Around him were other people, each of whom was looking at the monument. Then Garvey felt it. Perhaps sensed it was a better way of saying it. The others around him seemed to dissipate into the early afternoon air, all but Gramps. And Garvey, not quite knowing why he said it, heard himself saying --- "And will you speak to me, too? "

And then it happened again.

"Good to see you, Garvey. I was hoping you would come by after seeing those fellas over at the 555th monument. I can't add much to what 1st Sgt. Morris already said. It's always good to have visitors. People who remember us... As you know, we didn't jump out of airplanes. I was in the Civil War. Trying to end slavery. Trying to keep the Union strong. Not like the Buffalo soldiers who rode across the plains protecting the settlers in their covered wagons from --- what do you call them today? Native-Americans ---who were on the warpath... And who could blame them?

We sort of found ourselves in the middle. The "first people" ---- I like that term --- wanted to protect their lands. The settlers wanted a new start in the west, a chance to build a sod cabin, farm a few acres, and raise a family. Not much to ask for really. The Indians wanted about the same thing, though tents replaced sod and hunting trumped farming. Those guys did the best to keep the peace. Wasn't easy.

"I'm not sure we always had the "spirit, courage, and valor" that you folks believe we had. Kind of you to write those words on this monument... We were just guys doing our best. Sometimes that's enough...

"I don't want to keep you. Old Morris and I are together now, just pages in the history book. We'll remember your visit. And take care of your grandfather. He's made a long trip to visit us. We were expecting him to visit us for a long time.

"Garvey, you've got that look on your face again. "
"What look?"
" More voices?"
"Just the wind, Gramps."
"You're sure?"

There was no way Garvey was going to get into that one. No way at all. Whatever was going on was beyond him, and not something to be shared with others unless, of course, you didn't mind people looking at you funny. Yet, he was troubled. Twice now the voices had reminded him that Gramps had made a long trip. What was that about? And Gramps had said he and Garvey were expected without an explanation. Expected? How could that be? Again, another unanswered question.

"Then let's head back to the hotel. We've got an early flight tomorrow."

THE NEXT DAY

"Thirty minutes to go, Gramps."

"Fast flight."

"You slept the whole way."

"An advantage of being elderly."

"We need to talk."

"Is there a topic sentence here?"

"You heard them."

"Heard what?"

"The voices, Gramps."

Garvey couldn't let it go. He had tossed and turned in the motel bed unable to sleep, hearing the words again and again, *"Take care of your grandfather. He's made a long trip to visit us."* While waiting for their plane, and then, when once aboard, the words never left him. And then for some reason that movie --- *Field of Dreams* --- was running in his mind, competing for his attention. He could see Ray Kinsella staring at the cornfield, then at a star-studded sky, beseeching some distant deity for an answer. *"Who are you? What do you want?"* He could see Annie, Ray's fictional wife, supporting her husband, even his crazy idea to turn a valuable cornfield into a baseball diamond. He could see the fictional writer and philosopher, Terrence Mann, who had once been a civil rights activist pitting his pen against the ills of society. And "Doc" Graham, the very mysterious physician --- or was he a one-at-bat baseball player in the majors --- who bought his wife blue hats. He was also rummaging around in Garvey's thoughts. Why, he asked, had the film taken such a hold on him?

"Not that again, Garvey. Voices."

"Gramps, what's going on?"

"We did our best to keep the peace. Wasn't easy."

"You heard the voices!"

"Thought I was hallucinating. Happens to old guys, when they miss a pill."

"You didn't miss a pill. And we were expected. They knew we were coming."

"Who?"

"The monuments."

"That's silly."

"No, it's *Iowa*."

"What?"

"A place where dreams can come true."

"Nice place to visit."

"We did, Gramps."

Gramps looked at his grandson. The kid was curious, puzzled. The voices, he hadn't counted on that. Yes, he had schemed, plotted, and manipulated when the opportunity came. That wonderful research assignment had been the catalyst, the opportunity to finally keep a promise. And none to soon, given his age. But he hadn't counted on the voices. That was something else again. He knew he couldn't keep his grandson hanging any longer.

"Okay, Garvey, I'll come clean."

"We need to go back to 1945. Oakland, California. V.A. Hospital. My father, Samuel, your great-grandfather, was back from the war in the Pacific. U.S. Navy… He'd had a heart attack. He was an older man. Was in World War I; got called back for the sequel. Anyway, he ended up in Oak Knoll Veterans Hospital. Spent about two months there, along with wounded guys from all the services. They were all thrown together in vast wards of beds, nurses, and doctors, infantry, air force, navy --- the young and the once young --- the rich and the less so --- the educated and the near illiterate. It was a very democratic place.

"He saw lots of guys; there were beds on either side of his. New patients came and went, an endless march of wounded men. Though close-lipped about his own life my father was a good listener. People liked talking to him. He said little. They said a lot. They spoke. He nodded. Anyway, one day a young Black soldier was brought in. He had two broken legs to go with his equally broken right arm. The fella called himself Mike.

"They got to be friends. Maybe it was because my father stuck up for Mike when a couple of 'rednecks' said they didn't like Blacks mixed in with them. Stupid stuff… Why he did it, I'm not sure. Maybe, because he was Jewish, and heard similar crap about Jews --- "Christ-killers," "Jew bankers," or "war profiteers." Whatever… He told the "good old boys" off in no uncertain words.

"One day, Mike asked my father to write a letter for him to his folks back in Georgia. That's when my dad learned about Mike. He had been a member of some paratrooper outfit in Oregon, stationed in Pendleton. Mike referred to himself as a "Triple Nickel." A member of the 555th Airborne, an all-Black brigade in a segregated American military.

Of course, he had never heard of the balloon bombs, nor the 555th, and certainly any all-Black paratrooper group. Overtime, however, Mike shared the history of the 555th, and its logo. He became keenly interested in the unusual story.

"My father, Garvey, wanted to be a writer. Never had the chance beyond a couple of short stories, which were rejected. Needed to work to support his family. He just couldn't dedicate himself to the craft. As he listened to Mike, he realized what a great story this was, if only he could write it. He promised himself that he might. He never did.

"Just before my father was released from the hospital, Mike invited him to visit Atlanta, to meet his family. Dad made a promise to do it. He never did. Told me about the promises. Told me about his regrets, the book, and the trip. Promises made; promises unfulfilled. Asked me to do it someday. I sort of said I would."
"But you didn't."
"I didn't until… "
"The 555th assignment. Until this trip, Gramps?"
"Partially. We got to Kansas."

"You've kept your promise."

"With your help, Garvey, yes, partially."

"That's why we were expected?"

"Metaphorically speaking."

"And the voices, Gramps?"

"You tell me."

"We heard something."

"Our secret, Garvey."

"You could put it in the story your father never wrote, Gramps."

"At my age, no, but you could."

" Me!"

"You have a knack for writing. And this research paper is a good start."

"I..."

"No need to make a decision now... The book... Visiting his family someday... Got something to show you. Been carrying it around with me too long."

Gramps dug his hand deep into his inside jacket pocket. He pulled out an old envelope, a bit discolored, perhaps from water stains. He carefully lifted out a photograph and showed it to Garvey.

"Mike gave this to my father. Wanted him to have it. Said it would remind my father of him and his promise to visit. It was passed on to me. I'd like to give it to you. You can include it in your research and possible that unfinished book."

"Gramps..."

"Please..."

Garvey looked at the picture, long and hard. The entire 555th brigade was shown. It might have been a graduation photo. Perhaps it was... These men were paratroopers, all first in their class.

"They were so young, Gramps."

"And strong. Tall and strong and committed to 'kicking in doors.'"

"Which one is Mike?"

"I don't know. My father never told me. Always wondered about that."

"No hint?"

"None."

"Maybe they're all Mike, Gramps."

"Maybe."

CHAPTER 20

INTO HISTORY

The men were exhausted, almost beyond belief. But, of course, they would never admit to that. They were Army. They were paratroopers. They were smokejumpers.

The fire had tasked them, though, near to the breaking point.

Ignited by a lightning strike in the steeply graded foothills of the Siskiyou Forest, overgrown with thick underbrush below and towering ponderosa trees above, the fire had stubbornly resisted their efforts to contain it for five grueling days, chiseled into hours of blistering heat and nights of bone chilling cold. Five desperate days, a lifetime for these men…

The fire, an implacable foe, immune to the concerns of the seventeen men who had dropped out of the sky to contain it, simply roared and blazed, fed by an inexhaustible supply of fuel, and the presence of excessively low humidity, and increasingly gusty winds.

The fire was wild.

At first the men sought to flank the fire, initially clearing a three-foot path along its edge. On level terrain with only grass to contend with, how much easier it would have been. But on a slope, pitting a metal McLeod's blade and rake against the smooth, orange and red bark of the stiff, twisting branches of Manzanita, and rock filled top soil, proved no easy task. Even the dependable Polaski, part axe, part mattock, had trouble pushing aside shrubs stubbornly clinging to the soil.

Still, the men persisted. That was their job.

Ever so slowly, they squeezed the fire from a rounded-almond shape to what might be described as a narrowing Indian arrowhead, the tip of which was the flash point, the beating heart of the fire --- the front, which, like an unbroken stallion, might buck this way or that, changing direction, an uncontrollable, unpredictable creature lashing out with heated tongues of fire, nibbling at tree trunks, then inexorably climbing the oil-rich bark, seeking the tender-dried branches of the stately trees.

It wasn't until the fourth day that they could deal with the balloon bomb. They had trenched around the bomb, clearing a four-foot fire trail around it, just sufficient to keep the fire away. In short order, they defused the incendiaries before they could ignite. Those were tense moments, but no explosion, no casualties, and no fatalities. But it was never easy. There was always the shadow of a mishap and a blast. Cutting the wrong wire, a first and last mistake if it happened. But they had been trained, these Black paratroopers. They knew what they were doing.

On the fifth day, the men, now covered with soot and ash, now riddled with bug bites, now scraped and scratched, now smelling of smoke and their own sweat, got a break. They stumbled across a small cirque, a steep-sided hollow containing no more than two-feet of iced-water, too little to stop the fire, but sufficient to slacken tortured throats and to wash tired faces. Refreshed, the men again charged their relentless foe, no quarter given, nor asked, their tools no longer scraped and battered, but now bayonets glistening in the afternoon sun.

And then it was over. The fire was out, but at a price. Seventeen men had jumped. All answered the call to duty. None was unscathed by the fire.

Sgt. Bradley Biggs had a severely strained right ankle. His buddy, Walter Morris slid down an embankment, breaking little, and skinning a lot. Privates Calvin R. Beal, Clarence H. Beavers, and Hubert Bridges had multiple cuts and skin-stinging scratches. Servicemen Ned D. Bess, Lonnie M. Duke, and Robert Greene were treated for heat exhaustion. Officers Clifford Allen and Edward Baker were hit by falling branches, which almost knocked them out cold. Only their leather football helmets had prevented this. Paratroopers Wesby and Daniel C. Weil, and their buddy Roger S. Walden were overcome with choking blinding smoke, and almost coughed out their lungs. Smokejumpers James E. Kornegay, Alvin L. Moon, and Leo D. Reed had first-degree burns. Jack D. Tillis fell on his tailbone, while Samuel W. Robinson stubbed his big toe, both injuries privately painful, and publically funny.

The eleven-mile trek to Elk City took the men two-and-a-half days. Down from the timberline on paths goats would have shied away from, then on dirt lumber roads, dusty, dry, and drab, before finally reaching a curving, civilized two-lane road. Covered in ash and encrusted in dust, the men had a ghost-like quality, as if they didn't exist.

Less than half-a-mile from town, the men stopped. Helmets were removed. Faces were washed with the last of their canteen water. Equipment was fastened more securely. In teams of two, the men padded each other with worn blankets, removing what dust and grime they could from their uniforms.

They were soldiers. They would look like soldiers when they reached town. They would walk with pride. They would command respect. They were the "Triple Nickles."

What they had done, they would do again. More fires awaited them. That they knew. And what they did was done in the anonymity of a super-secret military program, unknown to the public, almost totally unrecognized within the Army. They wondered if this was their lot, to be lost in the pages of history.

But if the story of the 555th Paratroopers were ever known would anyone even care?

SEATTLE 2029

The University of Washington today published a book entitled *Leaping into the Sky*. The story is about the all-Black 555th paratroopers during World War II. The author was Garvey Langston, a high school senior. The book included an introduction by Professor Josiah Richmond, the head of the history department at the University. He was quoted, saying, "This book should be read by any young person on campus interested in understanding many crucial moments in America's racial history."

NO LONGER FORGOTTEN